Phalaenopsis Henriette Lecoufle 'Boule de Neige,' FCC/RHS. When awarded in November 1970 this plant had five pairs of leaves, two branched spikes of perfect 4-inch white flowers, 38 open blooms and 11 buds. The cross is Lachesis x Ramona. It has various forms of Phal. amabilis in its ancestry 23 times, Phal. stuartiana 4 times and Phal. schilleriana twice.

YOU CAN GROW PHALAENOPSIS ORCHIDS

By **MARY NOBLE**

Paintings by

Marion Ruff Sheehan

A sequel to:

YOU CAN GROW ORCHIDS

YOU CAN GROW CATTLEYA ORCHIDS

Published by:

Mary Noble

3003 Riverside Ave., Jacksonville, Florida, 32205 USA.

First edition.

Additional copies of the books in this series may be obtained from bookstores, orchid nurseries or garden stores or from the author, who is also the publisher, at the address on the preceding page.

CONTENTS

The Cover Flower: Phalaenopsis Mary Noble
Hybrid by Charles L. Beard

YOUR INTRODUCTION TO PHALAENOPSIS 7

I. THE PLANT AND ITS HABITS 9

II. ENVIRONMENT AND CARE 15

III. THE FLOWERS 29

IV. WHITE PHALAENOPSIS 35

V. PINK PHALAENOPSIS 47

VI. YELLOW PHALAENOPSIS 55

VII. NOVELTIES 61

VIII. TERETE PHALAENOPSIS 79

IX. RELATED GENERA 83

X. MULTIGENERICS 89

XI. POTTING AND REPOTTING 93

XII. PROPAGATION 97

XIII. PROBLEMS 105

XIV. DECORATIVE USE OF ORCHIDS 135

XV. CLASSIFICATION AND NOMENCLATURE 141

Recommended Reading 145

Acknowledgements and Photo Credits 145

Index 146

Map of Phalaenopsis Area .... Inside Back Cover

Dedicated to
Mr. and Mrs. Charles L. Beard
of West Palm Beach, Florida

**Phal. Scotti Maguire
'Gertie,' AM/AOS**

In 1951 Charlie Beard bought an orchid plant for his wife, Gertrude. But the more he read about orchids the more interested he became. Now the hobby is his, but many of the awarded clones carry the varietal name of 'Gertie.'

Charlie Beard specializes in phalaenopsis. He has produced many interesting and magnificent hybrids of superior quality. To this date his crosses have received more awards than those made by any other person.

This dedication is in appreciation of the Beards and their phalaenopsis flowers, which have added immeasurable beauty to many orchid collections around the world.

M.N.

YOUR INTRODUCTION TO PHALAENOPSIS

Phalaenopsis are exciting orchids. The Philippine people call them "mariposas" or butterflies. The name means "resembling a moth." The flowers look like fluttering winged creatures.

Besides the white phalaenopsis, which are favored for bridal bouquets, there are pink and yellow blooms, sunset-hued hybrids, and flowers of brown, purple, green and cream. Some have spots and stripes.

Originating mainly in the hot climates of the South Pacific, phalaenopsis are agreeable to growing on windowsills in high rise apartments, under trees in warm climate gardens, under lights in basements, or in greenhouses anywhere. The plants are attractive and the blooms numerous and durable. A dozen flowers on a stem may stay fresh for two months. What other potted plant can match this?

This book is the third in a series that began with YOU CAN GROW ORCHIDS, the basic book which gives information about orchids in general. Next is YOU CAN GROW CATTLEYA ORCHIDS. These subsequent titles go into more detail about the genera they discuss. By accumulating the books as they are published you will have a collection of references on the orchids most generally cultivated.

The aim of this book, as in those before it, is to help you—a hobby grower—to understand these orchids, to become acquainted with the many different phalaenopsis, and to grow them with success.

We orchid hobbyists are so numerous that we ring around the world but few of us are trained botanists. So we learn as we go and apply the information to our plants. And we share our knowledge and enthusiasm with each other.

A pastel design by Ruby Mack that you can copy. Put the pink phalaenopsis spray in a tube of water. Fill the green plastic vase with sand for weight. Use clipped umbrella plant for height, and a dried wisteria stem painted blue for line.

CHAPTER I

THE PLANT AND ITS HABITS

The important thing about growing a phalaenopsis or any other plant is to understand its structure and habits and then to supply its needs. If you know how it is put together you can help it grow.

A phalaenopsis plant is attractive, as orchid plants go. It has fleshy leaves arranged in a stairstep pattern.. If the plant is healthy the foliage is turgid but gracefully arched. The leaves may be solid green, or speckled above and purple below.

How The Plant Grows

A phalaenopsis plant is monopodial, meaning it has one foot (mono = one; pod = foot.) This is the opposite of a cattleya plant which is sympodial, has many feet, makes repetitious growths and moves sideways.

A phalaenopsis moves ever upwards. It has a single stem with leaves on the top and roots below or sometimes between the lower leaves.

A phalaenopsis plant has no pseudobulbs for storage of water and nutrients as does a cattleya type, but the succulent leaves have some storage ability. There are times when the phalaenopsis plant is making visible growth but it has no definite dormant or resting period because of limited storage to tide it over. Therefore, it should be kept growing all the time. Growth is negligible or slower when temperature and light are at a minimum so other factors must be balanced during such a period.

Parts of the Plant

LEAF — A seedling phalaenopsis plant is nothing but a pair of leaves above the potting mixture but even when small each plant shows its distinctive leaf design.

The leaf is large, rounded along the sides and rather flat. The size varies with the species and hybrids with the largest being those of Phalaenopsis gigantea. The normal size range for a mature plant is from 6 to 14 inches long and 2 to 4 inches wide. If a plant is well grown the newer leaves at the top are progressively larger than the seedling leaves at the bottom until mature size is reached.

Small-flowered species may have leaves 4 to 6 inches long and less than half that wide.

The leaf surface is smooth and waxy. The edges are smooth. Except for the rib down the center the longitudinal veins are visible only on close inspection, if then.

The leaf may be solid dark green, pale lime green or mottled with grey. It may be dark green with a reddish cast underneath, or as purple as an eggplant on the underside.

The new leaf emerges from the top center of the plant, first as a little green mouse ear folded in the middle. It grows upward then opens out and assumes a horizontal position. It generally arches gracefully about midway.

The mature leaf is slightly folded at the point where it joins the stem, which is its narrower end. The outer end may be round, pointed or somewhere between. Leaf outlines are described botanically as elliptic, oblong lanceolate, obovate, etc. A botany textbook or dictionary provides illustrations if you want to study further.

The leaves appear to be in pairs but are gradually staggered as they evolve one at a time but always opposite the previous leaf. A mature plant has several sets of leaves one above the other.

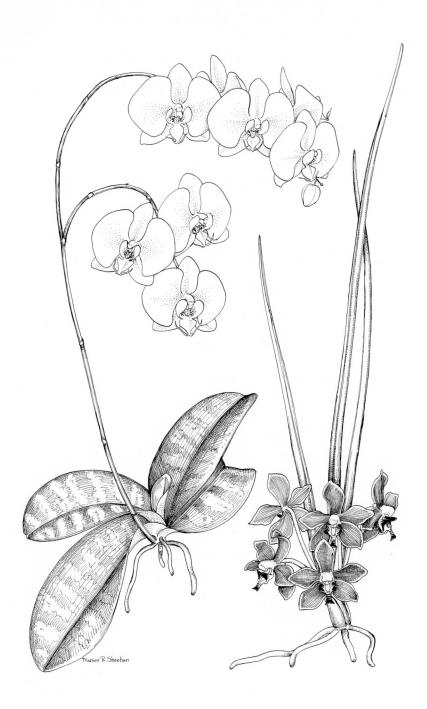

Marion R. Sheehan

Lower leaves gradually turn brown and fall off but if conditions are favorable a mature plant should retain four or five leaves most of the time. In the Philippines a well grown plant of P. schilleriana may have 10 leaves each 20 inches long.

A few species and their hybrids have terete or cylindrical leaves. See Chapter VIII.

STEM — The stem or central core of the plant is never visible as it is enclosed in the clasping bases of the leaves which wrap around it from one side and then the other. The newer leaf base overlaps the one below it. Even when a leaf falls off the break occurs where it slants out from the stem and the leaf base remains.

The apical meristem or growing point of the plant is inside the stem and is active indefinitely. The initiation of a flower spike from the side of the stem does not stop the plant from making new leaves from the crown, although no new leaves may be produced during flowering.

Along the side of the stem in the axil of each leaf are two tiny buds, sometimes three. They are hidden beneath the leaf bases and not visible and can be seen only under a microscope.

These buds are like little bumps, one on top of the other, which are capable of developing into vegetative or flowering parts. The buds remain quiescent until the environmental conditions induce the plant to flower, when the bud on top develops as a flower spike. The one or two underneath it do nothing unless stimulated into activity. (See Propagation Chapter.)

This characteristic of phalaenopsis differs from cattleyas in that a cattleya has only one bud at the top of its pseudobulb and once a pseudobulb has flowered it cannot do so again. However, some dendrobiums have extra dormant buds that flower or make keikis after the first flowering from that bulb.

INFLORESCENCE — The flower spike which rises from an active bud on the side of the stem grows sideways for a fraction of an inch and then bends up from under the side of the leaf and grows straight up. If it is long and heavy with flowers it arches pendantly and the end may be below the foliage. You may need to support a long flower stem with a horizontal wire, or elevate the plant on an upturned pot so the flowers hang free.

The inflorescence may be as thick as your finger or as thin as a strand of green spaghetti, depending on the nature of the ancestral species.

It may be very long in the case of mature plants, or quite short on seedlings. It may be flat with zig-zag edges. Doritis spikes grow straight up until they get very tall, then begin to curve and may be wrapped around and around as they elongate.

Some spikes continue to lengthen for months, blooming from the ends.

The inflorescence is a raceme or a panicle. The definition is an elongated flower spike with flowers bearing individual stalks. If it is branched it is a panicle.

The spike has a flowerless stretch at the base with five to seven nodes. A node is a joint or ring around the stem with a tiny green triangular bump on one side. This is a bud covered by a slightly larger green bract like a triangle of tissue paper which hugs the stem. Nodes may be an inch or more apart on the stem on alternate sides.

If the flowering part of the inflorescence is cut, when environmental conditions are favorable a secondary inflorescence may develop from one of these buds another season. These buds are capable of making new plants as keikis or mericlones. However, some types of phalaenopsis continue to produce flowers at the ends of the spikes at intervals and these spikes should not be cut.

ROOT — The root of a phalaenopsis plant is rather large. It is white or silver on the surface with green showing through. It has a translucent green or amber growing tip.

Roots are numerous and produced at the base of the stem, growing right through the leaf bases and sometimes appearing above the lower leaves.

A phalaenopsis root is round or flat depending on the plant's ancestry. It is a holdfast, and also a searcher for moisture and nutrients. It grows down in the container, round and round inside the rim, sometimes climbing up over the side of the pot to hang out in the air.

In nature a phalaenopsis plant perches in trees and the roots hold on tenaciously. They forage in the crevices of the bark. They become tangled with roots of other plants. If the limb falls, the plant may swing in the air, held aloft by some far-ranging roots on another limb. If the plant falls the roots penetrate the humus of the forest floor.

The structure of the phalaenopsis root is like that of other monocotyledonous roots, a series of circles one inside the other.

The central conducting cylinder is the stele in which the xylem and phloem carry water and carbohydrates up and down respectively. The

Phalaenopsis Samba is ivory circled with amethyst. (Phal. Star of Rio x Phal. amboinensis).

cortex layer around the stele is made up of cells containing chloroplasts. This is the location of the green color.

The velamen layer around the cortex is separated from it by a wall of single cells called the exodermis which lets water in but not out. The velamen layer is made up of large dead cells with thick walls to keep them from collapsing. The air in these cells makes the root look white or silver. The velamen layer works like a blotter. It absorbs moisture vapor and water from the air or potting mix and passes it to the inner root tissues.

Because the velamen can absorb moisture all along the length of the root, the phalaenopsis plant can lead an epiphytic existence. But the reverse is also true. The root must have air to function and so the potting mix must be open, and not so saturated with water that air is excluded.

The short colored root tip is the only part of the root that grows, being pushed constantly forward by a layer of dividing cells just behind the tip.

CHAPTER II

ENVIRONMENT AND CARE

If the environment is suitable to their way of life, phalaenopsis plants grow well and bloom gloriously.

The trick, as with all orchids, is to balance the factors against each other. More light calls for more of everything else: water, fertilizer and warmth. In cooler temperature ranges, restrained watering is not only needed but is imperative to avoid rot, and the light should not be so bright.

So, for success you need to consider all the factors in the environment in which your plants grow, whether this is the controlled environment of a greenhouse, on a windowsill in your home, or under lights indoors. Even in the rather uncontrollable conditions of a slat house or a garden, some modifications can be achieved if you locate plants in more or less sun, away from the wind, or under temporary cover in cold weather.

So what do your phalaenopsis want?

There are clues in the natural habitats where the plants grow wild, or did grow wild as most of them have long since been collected and brought into cultivation.

There are about 40 species in the genus Phalaenopsis native to an area that extends from China, Tibet and the Himalayas through Southeast Asia and the islands of the South Pacific into northern Australia. There's evidence from the similarity of the vegetation that these areas might have been linked together in some way in prehistoric times.

The general impression is that phalaenopsis (and all orchids for that matter) grow in jungles and rain forests where trees are tall, vegetation crowded and the air steaming. Apparently the phalaenopsis grow high up in trees perhaps 100 feet tall so as to get their share of rain and light. They are small plants by comparison with their companions—the huge trees and vines of the tropics, and would be crowded out of existence if they grew down low. Often they are found near the seacoast, usually in the shade or semi-shade of thin-leaved trees and always where the air moves. Inland they are found near mountain streams where the air is humid and in motion.

Altitude is a factor in considering natural habitats. It is not enough to say that a species comes from the Philippines because that chain of 7,000 islands extends over 1,000 miles. The topography is mostly mountainous, some up to 9,000 feet. Most of the orchids grow between 1,500 and 6,000 feet. Temperature varies with altitude, being quite low at times in the higher mountains. The duration of the wet and dry seasons varies with the geography.

For example, at Surigao on the Philippine Island of Mindanao, the home of Phal. stuartiana, there is no dry season. The mean minimum temperature ranges from 72° to 75°F. year round, but this is the average. The mean maximum is from 84° to 90°F. and the rainfall from four to 25 inches per month. The mean relative humidity is 79 to 88 percent. The average percentage of the sky covered with clouds is 58 to 74 percent during the day.

Phal. schilleriana, indigenous to Quezon Province on Luzon, flowers profusely in winter in its native habitat or in mountainous regions elsewhere, but in Manila where the temperature is higher (73° to 89°F.) and there is a six months dry period it may produce keikis instead of flowers.

The contemporary hybrids are such mixtures of several species that they are adaptable to a reasonably suitable environment. However, if a plant is not doing well and there is no visible pest or disease problem, trace its parentage to see if the species from which it derives are limited in range to low or high altitudes, warm or cool climates and adjust the plant's environment as much as possible within your growing area. Even a slight variation in temperature or light may make a difference in its happiness.

Temperature

Most phalaenopsis come from warm climates and therefore need to be grown warm. The air needs to move and be fresh, not heavy and stifling.

How warm? The islands of the South Pacific get hot at times and phalaenopsis can, too. But if the temperature is high the air must be moving and moist. They can take it in the 90's for short periods. A range between 65° and 85°F. by day is desirable. If the temperature is high, the air dry and the light bright, the plants dry out too rapidly to function.

How cool? Most writers say to keep the night temperature above 60°F. This is the safe figure. On the other hand, low night temperatures (within reason) help to initiate buds. This is the way commercial growers get their phals to bloom all year round, maybe four crops of flowers annually. In California a drop to 55°F. for three or four weeks causes spikes to initiate within a month. Flowers begin to open within 90 days and the full spike is generally open in 120 days.

In tropical climates, a drop down to 60°F. at night by the use of cooling equipment initiates the spikes. And in South Florida, Charlie Beard puts plants in summer in the cool room of his greenhouse which gets down to 68°F. at night and up to 74°F. by day and he has a house full of flowers in the fall. Once the spikes show he moves the plants into the regular greenhouse. However, new spikes initiated for fall blooming have flowers smaller than the winter and spring crop, more like those produced on secondary spikes. You could do the same by bringing plants into an air conditioned room to chill them.

In their native habitats, the average temperatures may be steady all year, but there is a drop of about 15 degrees between day and night.

Phalaenopsis flower magnificently and almost constantly on the California coast where the fogs roll in at night and chill the air.

You don't want to keep your phalaenopsis so nice and warm that they do not flower. One year I had a new heater that was so efficient the temperature stayed in the high 60's and many of my phals did not flower until summer. The buds for that were triggered by a cool spell in the spring after I had turned off the heat for the season. I have no cooling system, but I open all the doors and vents.

If there is a late cool spell in the spring and you turn your thermostat lower, or if your phals are outside in the warmer climates and the temperature drops, the plants will send up secondary spikes from the stubs of the spikes you have cut and often initiate new spikes as well.

As houseplants in a heated room phals may not flower if the temperature is constantly high. Put them where you can lower the night temperature to set the buds.

On the other hand, once flowers have opened, low night temperatures may cause sepal wilt or botrytis spotting. See Problem Chapter.

In Europe some phalaenopsis are grown at a minimum of 65°F. (18°C.) and the vents not opened when the outside temperature is below 72°F. But if the minimum is dropped to 60°F. the plants bloom twice a year. Once spikes appear in the fall the commercial ranges may run temperatures at 76°F. night and day to provide a Christmas crop of flowers.

Amateur growers in cold climates can grow phalaenopsis with paphiopedilums at a range between 50°F. at night and 63°F. or thereabouts by day. Very careful watering is required in the winter as plant growth is slowed almost to dormancy. Such plants bloom in summer instead of spring.

How cool? I have had my plants outdoors at 40°F. for short periods and they suffered no injury.

Any temperature changes should be gradual. Phalaenopsis do not like cold drafts, cold water, or wet feet or wet foliage when it is cold. They don't like an air conditioner blowing right on them either.

Light and Shade

Sunlight is the source of energy for the process of photosynthesis by which any plant lives and grows. All the oxygen we breathe is produced by green leaves. (For more about photosynthesis see YOU CAN GROW CATTLEYA ORCHIDS.)

Plants can be grown under artificial lights instead of sunlight. Artificial lights can be combined with daylight to supplement it in areas where there are many dull days or air pollution reduces the daylight. If you grow orchids in a greenhouse where there are less than six hours of bright daylight, consider installing artificial lights to supplement the sun. See section later in this chapter.

Phalaenopsis growers vary in their recommendations of light for phalaenopsis from 700 foot candles to 3,000.

Phalaenopsis can take much more light than was thought for a long time provided the other factors are in balance. With brighter light you must provide higher humidity, moving air, and adequate fertilizer and water to sustain the plants.

Adequate light is important to produce strong plants and strong flower stems with the maximum number of blooms. Direct sunlight is generally too strong and leaves will burn quickly but many amateurs with a single greenhouse grow phalaenopsis along with cattleyas and vandas in the 3,000 foot candle range.

Seedlings should have less light than mature plants. Their foliage is more tender and their small pots dry out more rapidly.

Warm humid air that moves helps to cool the leaf surfaces and prevent burning and light can be stronger than in a situation where the air is dry and still.

If shade is too dense the foliage is limp and the flowers are soft. Plants may not bloom, and there is danger of rot.

If the light is too bright and fertilizer, water and temperature not sufficient to encourage maximum growth, the foliage may be hard and stunted. If the light is bright but the humidity is low, leaves shrivel.

Watch your plants to determine their needs. As long as the foliage is growing and is crisp and sturdy, probably the light is right.

In the dull days of winter or during long periods of cloudy days or air pollution, plants may languish in the diminished light but should perk up when conditions improve.

If you grow under a plastic roof, observe it for gradual darkening as plastic deteriorates in ultraviolet light. Different plastic materials age differently and the light levels change each year, perhaps 20 percent reduction. Plastic and glass both get dirty and should be scrubbed inside and out once a year.

If in doubt use a light meter that registers in foot candles when your plants are doing well and make readings periodically thereafter.

Feel your foliage at midday when the seasons are changing. If a leaf is hot to the touch it is in danger of burning. Either lower the temperature by ventilation, reduce the light by temporary shading, or reduce the leaf temperature by misting it with water.

Houseplants

Phalaenopsis are excellent houseplants because they can exist with reasonable light conditions. They grow on a windowsill or in a room with lots of glass, or under artificial lights.

The plant is attractive, as orchid plants go. The flowers are showy and long lasting. It is easy to see why a pot of phalaenopsis easily outperforms such conventional houseplants as African violets and philodendrons.

I once had a phalaenopsis plant in bloom delivered to the ship for friends departing on a cruise. It graced their stateroom all during the trip, provided corsage flowers for special occasions, and came home with the travelers to grow and bloom in succeeding years.

For houseplants east or south windows are desirable and morning sun is essential. If the sun is too bright, lower a blind or curtain at midday. If you are not home all day, experiment on weekends by following the sun's path and feeling the foliage. If leaves get hot, move plants away from the windows. Watch plants as the seasons and the sun's angle change and the trees outside shed or grow leaves.

The setup for growing phalaenopsis under artificial lights is the same as for other orchids.

Use four 40-watt tubes of mixed wide-spectrum and daylight fluorescent tubes over each shelf. These provide about 1,000 to 1,200

Dr. and Mrs. J. F. duPlooy of Johannesburg, South Africa, grow phalaenopsis and other orchids in a greenhouse built with the foundation below the ground to help lower the temperature.

foot candles of light at the center, 800 or less at the ends. Replace the tubes as their intensity diminishes with age. Use a light meter to check the consistency.

Some growers recommend an additional four 25-watt incandescent bulbs spaced evenly apart. Commercial extended service 130-volt bulbs last longer than standard 120-volt incandescent bulbs.

If your collection is of mixed genera, experiment with location to see which plants do best in the center where the light is brighter than at the end of the rows.

Stage phalaenopsis about 12 inches below the lights. Burn the lights 12 to 16 hours per day. Install an automatic timer to turn them on and off.

Water and Humidity

Phalaenopsis grow where afternoon showers are usual, sometimes torrential, but brief. In many of their habitats the sun shines in the morning, clouds gather and rain falls in the afternoon and the sky clears in time for the sunset.

This indicates that phalaenopsis need frequent and ample watering, moist air, and rapid drying off.

In cultivation daily watering of mature plants is seldom necessary unless the light is very bright. Roots are confined in pots instead of strung along tree limbs; plants are crowded on greenhouse benches instead of perched in treetops, and potting material is slower to dry out than exposed tree bark.

The clue is obvious. Water only enough to keep your plants moist. In cool weather water early in the day so foliage dries off before night.

There are no set rules. Small pots of seedlings need almost daily attention. Hanging baskets dry off faster than plastic or clay pots. Large plants in eight-inch pots may need watering only once a week when the temperature is low.

Again it is a matter of balance. If the air is warm and moving the evaporation of moisture from the leaves is more rapid than when the air is chilly and still.

Overwatering is bad for any type of orchid as it crowds out the air around the roots, and without air they can't function.

A lot depends on the type and condition of the potting material. If it is soft and holds water, water less often than if it is crisp and

Mr. Malcolm Gray of Suva, Fiji, grows phalaenopsis under a plastic roof to protect the flowers from heavy rains.

porous. Roots rot in soggy compost, but need to be moist all the time. When you water, do it thoroughly so water runs through the pot and out the drainage holes freely. Don't be timid. Pouring a little water on the surface does nothing for roots down below nor does it wash out fertilizer salts.

Tote your indoor plants to a sink or bathtub to water them thoroughly and leave them to drain.

Mr. and Mrs. Jean Paul Jones grow orchids in their prefab glass greenhouse in Jacksonville, Florida.

Check the temperature of the water. It should be as warm as the air in cool temperatures, but cooler in hot weather.

In cool weather do not get water in the crown of the plant. If it stands long, it will cause rot. Some growers hang their phalaenopsis sideways so water runs off the top.

Phalaenopsis are almost always in growth except when their environment is cold and they have no definite resting period when water should be withheld. Water sparingly when the temperature is low.

HUMIDITY — This is a different thing from water in the pot. The relative humidity is the amount of water vapor in the air expressed as a percentage of the maximum amount that the air could hold at a given temperature.

Phalaenopsis have wide succulent leaves that are full of water. Dry air causes this water to evaporate from leaves into the air, and in extreme conditions or over long periods, causes the leaves to wilt. You can inject humidity into the air by use of humidifying equipment in a greenhouse, mist sprinklers above the benches, or by misting plants with the garden hose fitted with a mist nozzle.

You can increase humidity around indoor plants by setting them above pans of water. Use metal racks above the level of the water so plants do not touch it. Use some kind of hand mister to apply moisture to houseplants.

Artificial heat and air conditioners dry out the air, calling for more frequent efforts to raise the relative humidity.

Lower humidity is desirable when air pollution is severe.

Nutrients

The amount of fertilizer, the type and the frequency you use depend on all the other factors of the environment and the type of potting material.

Whatever brand you choose, dilute and apply exactly as specified. If you apply it more often, dilute it proportionately. Flush plants thoroughly with clear water at regular intervals to remove excess fertilizer salts that burn roots.

Fertilize phalaenopsis planted in bark mixtures with 30-10-10. For plants in other mixtures use a balanced formula like 18-18-18, 20-20-20 or 14-14-14. Apply about every 10 to 14 days when plants are in active growth, perhaps every 21 days when growth is slower in cool weather, or when the sky overcast or the air polluted.

Foliar feeding is beneficial. I do most of my fertilizing this way. It is easy and quick. I use a soluble fertilizer and dilute about half the strength recommended for pot applications, and apply it with a mist sprayer to the foliage. I use the same spray equipment that I do for pest control, a plastic bottle with a thin hose and adjustable nozzle, a handle to pump up the air pressure. One gallon mists the foliage of about 100 phals.

I am of the opinion that two or three applications of 5-30-30 to the pot when the temperature is lowered helps to initiate the spikes.

Pelletized fertilizer releases nutrients slowly from a plastic shell. Use this material in the same formula as a rapidly soluble fertilizer. If you also use a soluble fertilizer, then apply pellets in half the recommended amount and dilute the soluble to half the recommended strength. Apply new granules as directed. Most of these pellets last two to three months, depending on temperature, water and other factors.

I think an occasional application of a liquid organic is excellent if you do not use this all the time. If you can get pasture manure and soak it to make "cow tea" and then dilute it so it is almost colorless and pour it on the pots, it gives plants a boost. Liquid fish emulsion is very good for orchids. For the formula for "violet water" made of poultry manure, see chapter on White Phalaenopsis.

European growers who plant phalaenopsis in two parts live sphagnum to one part polypodium fiber (osmunda) add some dried cow manure to the mixture but caution against watering with manure water as too much manure kills the growing sphagnum.

I have mixed well-rotted (never fresh) cow manure with tree fern chunks and the phals grew vigorously in it. Packaged dehydrated manure is more concentrated and if you use it, just sprinkle a little on the surface when potting.

You can sprinkle a little dried blood or bone meal on the pot surface once or twice a year. Blood is nine to 14 percent nitrogen and bone meal is three to four percent nitrogen, released slowly.

In Hawaii, May and Goodale Moir grow their phalaenopsis in 75 to 80 percent sunlight and give them small amounts of liquid fertilizer at almost every watering, daily in normal weather but not at all when it rains. The foliar fertilizer brands are rotated so one type cannot build up an accumulation of certain salts. They use plain water regularly to wash out the salts.

When they repot they add a small amount of organic fertilizer to the compost and give a second application when the plant shows a spike.

If the leaves are leathery and plants growing in bright light the Moirs make a daily application when plants are developing their spikes of a mixture of one teaspoon foliar fertilizer and two teaspoons sugar to one gallon of water.

Caution: don't move your plants suddenly into 80 percent sunlight, and don't give a daily dose of the above formula unless you have all

Mr. Charles L. Beard stages some phalaenopsis on horizontal pipes as well as on benches in his suburban greenhouse.

the other factors of light, warmth, and humidity. However, in less light you can apply the fertilizer-sugar mixture to plants less often.

(Note: the Moirs grow paphiopedilums with their phalaenopsis and say they love the bright light and constant feeding.)

Another use for this fertilizer-sugar mixture, they say, is for dipping newly imported plants. First wash off the residue of the fumigation, then soak plants in the sugar solution for 30 minutes before potting. It revives the green color. Dip plants upside down in the mixture every few days until they begin to grow.

Air Quality

Besides the temperature and humidity of the air around phalaenopsis, two other factors are important. Circulation and pollution.

Pollution is a problem with flowers rather than plants as far as we know and is discussed in the Problem Chapter. However, some of the mysterious leaf problems that don't check out as diseases or pests may be due to pollution.

Remember that phalaenopsis grow high in trees where the breezes are brisk. They like moving air. Stagnant air lets moisture stay on foliage and flowers and brings on rots of the foliage and botrytis on the flowers.

There are several ways to move air. Turbulators or fans in closed greenhouses move the air. In a small greenhouse without cooling equipment, open the door and a top vent to make the air move. In cold weather less than freezing, open a roof vent at the far end of the house from the heater to move a current of air through the house. Hot air rises. In the summer, open everything unless you live in a very dry area where humidity is very low.

An excellent device for distributing air in a large greenhouse is a polyethylene convection tube extending the length of the house and perforated with two and one-half inch holes at intervals. A fan at one end to blow air in or an exhaust fan to suck it out circulates the air in the greenhouse evenly without drafts. This equipment can be used for circulating heat, carbon dioxide or pesticides.

CHAPTER III

THE FLOWERS

The name phalaenopsis indicates that the flower looks like a moth (Phalen = moth, opsis = appearance.)

It is believed that the pollinators of phalaenopsis are night-flying insects, perhaps moths, for the white-flowered species stand out glistening against the darkness of night like pearls on black velvet. Surely this attracts the pollinators.

The basic composition of all orchid flowers is repeated in the phalaenopsis blooms.

SEPALS — There are three sepals, alike as to size and shape. These are the three outer segments that are the outside of the bud. On the open flower they form a triangle. The sepal at the top is the dorsal sepal and it may be slightly larger than the two lateral or ventral sepals.

On the large-flowered types descended from Phal. amabilis, Phal. schilleriana and Phal. stuartiana the sepals are narrower than the petals. In other species such as Phal. lueddemanniana and Phal. cornu-cervi and similar small-flowered types, the sepals are equal to or even wider than the petals.

Show schedules often divide the phalaenopsis classes by headings: "Petals broader than sepals," and "Petals equal to or narrower than sepals."

The sepals are generally of the same base color as the petals but the two lower sepals may have extra spotting or color repetitious of that in the lip. It often appears only on the inner half of these sepals.

PETALS — There are three petals. Two of these are spread like wings and are a matched pair. The third is the curious sixth segment that is different from the other five segments and is the lip.

The petals may be flat or slightly turned at an angle.

They may be similar to the sepals in color and markings, or lacking some of the extra color found on the lower sepals.

TEPALS — When the sepals and the two identical petals are similar in form and color they may be referred to collectively as tepals.

LIP — The lip of a phalaenopsis flower varies considerably from the other segments and from species to species.

The lip always has three lobes, some very distinct. The front lobe is usually a curious shape. Only Mother Nature could have designed it. The two lobes more or less frame the column but do not enclose it as do the side lobes of a cattleya-type orchid lip.

The lip has raised lines or callus-like bumps between the two side lobes and below the column, presumably to guide the pollinating insect so he comes in contact with the column above either to pick up or deliver pollen.

Examine the fascinating lip designs in our illustrations and on your own flowers. The midlobe, which projects forward or downward may be shaped like a teardrop (Phal. lindenii), like a shovel (Phal. lueddemanniana), or like an anchor (Phal. stuartiana). In the case of Phal. parishii it is a hinged crescent that wiggles.

Also distinctive are the tendrils that appear at the ends of the midlobes of some species, notably Phal. amabilis on which they are long and curling.

Some lips, as on Phal. fimbriata, have clumps of hairs.

Lips are distinctive in color. In the white flowers the lip is usually marked with yellow. There are white phalaenopsis with red or rosy lips. On some of the striped flowers the lip is a solid color. Often it is marked on the lobes with solid color or spots. There is often concentrated color in the area of the callus.

COLUMN — The column, which is club-shaped, is a distinguishing feature of all orchids. It is in the center of the flower where all the segments meet and it contains all the reproductive parts of the flower. The anther is like a cap on the front of the column, easily dislodged to remove the pollen. The two yellow pollen grains of pinhead size and

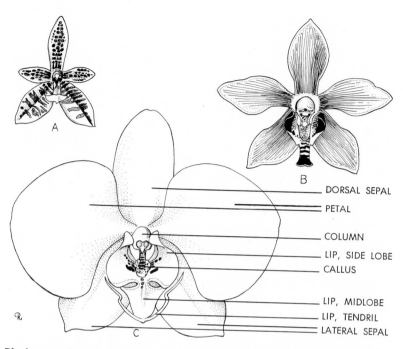

DORSAL SEPAL

PETAL

COLUMN

LIP, SIDE LOBE

CALLUS

LIP, MIDLOBE

LIP, TENDRIL

LATERAL SEPAL

Phalaenopsis flower types. A. Phal. cornu-cervi; B. Phal. denevei; C. Phal. sanderiana.

called pollinia, are located behind the anther. Next comes a partition called the rostellum which prevents self-pollination by separating the pollen, or male part, from the stigma, or female part. The stigma is a cavity behind the rostellum which- is lined with a sticky substance to which the pollen sticks when inserted in the cavity.

The phalaenopsis column, being fully exposed, may be the same color as the petals or the lip or may be white.

OVARY — Each bloom has an individual stem which attaches it the main inflorescence. This stem is called a pedicel and it contains the ovary. So when the flower is pollinated the stem back of the flower swells into the seed pod.

INFLORESCENCE — The main stem to which the pedicels are attached is discussed in Chapter I.

Good Qualities of Flowers

You need not have only award winning flowers in your collection. If you like them that is all that matters. But when making a choice consider the points the judges score for awards.

This is the American Orchid Society's scale for measuring flower quality of phalaenopsis blooms. The number of points for each value is based upon the quality of each flower according to its inheritance. Naturally a flower one generation removed from Phal. mannii will not be similar in size to one once removed from Phal. amabilis. Each one is considered according to its own potential.

FORM — 30 points. The large white and pink phals have developed almost perfect form as well as maximum size. In these types the ideal flower is flat, the segments overlap so there is no space between petals and sepals, and the silhouette is round or oval.

Other types are decidedly star shaped, pointed or rounded on the ends of the segments. The lip varies according to variety.

The overall flower should be well balanced. The sepals should be arranged in an equilateral triangle.

COLOR — 30 points. The color of a good flower is clear and pleasing. White flowers should be opaque clear white, not dingy. Markings, such as spots or stripes, should be definite and arranged in an attractive pattern. The lip should be distinctive as to color, preferably brighter than the tepals. The color of a solid flower should extend all the way to the edges of the segments. In flowers where there is a suffusion of one color over another, as in some of the sunset shades, the effect should be harmonious and not muddy.

SIZE — 10 points. To win an award the size of an individual flower should be equal to the average size of the parents, or larger. While size carries visual weight with many people, note that it is only 10 points. Emphasis is on color and form. Larger size calls for better balance so the flower scores well on form. A plant must be grown well to produce flowers of desirable size.

In some types of breeding the aim is to miniaturize the progeny. Phalaenetia (Phalaenopsis x Neofinetia) would be scored on an average

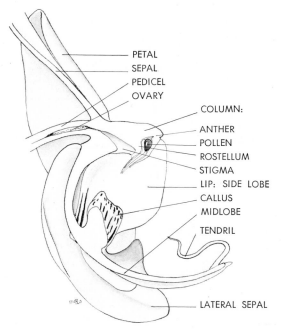

PETAL
SEPAL
PEDICEL
OVARY
COLUMN:
ANTHER
POLLEN
ROSTELLUM
STIGMA
LIP: SIDE LOBE
CALLUS
MIDLOBE
TENDRIL
LATERAL SEPAL

Cross section of phalaenopsis flower.

size between the two parents, and not expected to equal the larger parent. Likewise, Doriella (Kingiella x Doritis) blooms much smaller than the larger parent.

SUBSTANCE AND TEXTURE — 10 points. Substance is the crispness of the flower, a quality to feel with the fingertips more than to see. Any phalaenopsis worth having in a collection should have good substance and hold its segments up and never look floppy.

Texture is a surface quality, which should never be dull. In white phals the surface should sparkle.

HABIT AND ARRANGEMENT OF INFLORESCENCE — 10 points. For sprays of large whites and pinks the flowers should be placed like shingles, evenly spaced and barely touching or overlapping. All the flowers on the same side of a stem should face the same way. One that turns is out of step. In other lines of breeding the habit and arrangement vary.

No need to throw out a plant because it one time produces an awkward spike or flowers that twist the wrong direction. Next time it may be perfect.

FLORIFEROUSNESS — 10 points. This concerns the number of flowers and depends upon heredity and culture. A well grown plant should produce a maximum number of blooms for its type.

The points required for American Orchid Society awards are: First Class Certificate (F.C.C.) 90 to 100 points; Award of Merit (A.M.), 80 to 89 points; Highly Commended Certificate (H.C.C.) 75-79 points.

Other organizations have other requirements. The Australian Orchid Council uses the same scale of points, but the figures for the various awards are different. They require that the points for form average not less than a certain percentage of the possible points. They define the size scale by inches, with a phalaenopsis flower 4 3/4 inches and over allowed 10 points, one less than 3 inches no points. They define a scale for floriferousness beginning at 10 points for 20 flowers or more and only three points for seven flowers, with less than that not eligible for consideration.

CHAPTER IV

WHITE PHALAENOPSIS

The contemporary white phalaenopsis have a remarkable ancestor in the species Phalaenopsis amabilis.

The man who named it mistook the spray of flowers for a cluster of white butterflies and recorded it as Phalaenopsis amabilis, from the Latin for "looking like lovely moths."

Imagine if you can the fascination of this Dutch botanist, Dr. C. L. Blume. It was about 1825 and he was Director of the Royal Botanic Gardens, Buitenzorg, Java. He was out exploring for plants, some say on the island of Noesa Kembangan just south of Java. It was virgin territory with no trails and in the oppressive afternoon heat of the jungle he was climbing up a mountain slope on a rocky river bed. He saw lots of orchids but all familiar species.

While resting on a rock he was watching the many swarms of brightly colored butterflies above the water through his field glasses, and on the opposite bank he was surprised to see a group of about 20 dazzling white butterflies hovering almost motionless near a tree.

He scrambled over rocks to get closer, and was amazed to find that they were not butterflies but orchids!

Native collectors were sent later to bring the plant to the Botanical Garden. Dr. Blume described his new genus Phalaenopsis in "Bijdragen Tot de Flora van Nederlandsch Indie" published in 1825. In botanical writing today the genus name is followed by Blume's name.

However, Phalaenopsis amabilis had been seen by other men and given other names prior to this incident.

A great 17th century German botanist named G. E. Rumphius found a plant of it growing on the Spice Island of Ambon (Amboina) and published a description of it in 1750 in the sixth volume of "Herbarium Amboinense." He called it Angraecum album majus. This was the Latinized form of the native name, "Anggrek Boelan" which means "moon orchid."

Peter Osbeck was en route from China to England on a ship that stopped at New Island at the western end of Java on January 19, 1752, to take on water. He went ashore, carried over the coral reefs on the shoulders of wading seamen. He pushed aside foliage to make his way into the wet dark rain forest, reporting that the forest was so noisy with birds, lizards and other screaming creatures that the men could not hear themselves talk. On branches near the shore he collected some orchids. He dried the plants and took them to Europe to Linnaeus (the Swedish botanist who devised the system of genus and species names.) All the epiphytic orchids known to Linnaeus at that time were classed as Epidendrum, so he described this new find in "Species Plantarum" in 1753 as Epidendrum amabile.

Apparently the phalaenopsis flowers were appreciated by the natives of the islands on which they grew. Osbeck noted that on the Isle of Ternate only princesses were allowed to wear them.

In 1798 plants from the Moluccas were sent to the Botanic Gardens at Calcutta and were reclassified as Cymbidium by Dr. Roxburgh in 1814 in "Flora Bengalensis."

So, variously called Angraecum, Epidendrum and Cymbidium, Blume's name of Phalaenopsis finally won out.

Phalaenopsis amabilis now embraces those previously named Phal. aphrodite, Phal. formosa or formosana, Phal. rimestadiana and Phal. grandiflora. It is widely distributed through the South Pacific from Queensland, Australia to Taiwan.

PHALAENOPSIS AMABILIS — It has flowers from 3 to 5 inches wide, petals broader than sepals, milky white sometimes tinged pink on the back. The lip is narrow, white with golden yellow and crimson touches and has long curled tendrils. There are many flowers on a cylindrical, arching spike.

The foliage is clear bright green, generously rounded and sometimes tapering at the base. On specimen plants each leaf may be 18 to 20

Phalaenopsis stuartiana.

inches long, but a more general range is 12 inches long and 4 inches wide.

Let's look at the plants now regarded as Phal. amabilis which were formerly distinct species.

PHALAENOPSIS APHRODITE — Whatever its status botanically the name is appropriate because Aphrodite was the Greek goddess of beauty.

A live plant of Phal. aphrodite reached England in 1837 sent from Manila by collector Hugh Cuming. Only one plant survived the long sea voyage and it bloomed for Messrs. Rollisson in Tooting in the fall of that year. It was the model for Dr. Lindley's illustration of Phal. amabilis in the "Botanical Register'" in July 1838.

Apparently this was the first phalaenopsis plant to bloom in Europe some 87 years after Rumphius had seen one in the wild.

Phalaenopsis aphrodite was discovered by a Jesuit Brother, George Joseph Kamel, who was interested in plants and able to draw. Phal. aphrodite was among the first plants he reported from the Philippines in "Historis Plantarum" in 1704. A drawing published in 1709 in another publication is preserved in the British Museum of Natural History.

Phal. aphrodite (now Phal. amabilis) has smaller flowers than other varieties of the species, about three inches wide. The leaves are 12 inches or more long with prominent midribs, green on top and purplish below.

The white flowers sometimes have a flush of green or cream near the center of the flower, or tiny reddish dots on the inner halves of the lateral sepals. It flowers throughout the year in the Philippines.

PHALAENOPSIS FORMOSANA (formosa, formosiana) − Now also Phal. amabilis, comes from Taiwan, is pure white with no color on the back of the blooms or underneath the leaves. The plant is smaller, about 8 inches maximum leaf length.

PHALAENOPSIS RIMESTADIANA − This is a variety with large pure white flowers without color on the back. The blooms have heavier substance and longer durability than the other whites. Now Phal. amabilis var. rimestadiana.

PHALAENOPSIS GRANDIFLORA − It comes from the southern tip of Palawan, the westernmost point of the Philippine Islands where the flora is distinctive. It has large flowers, up to 5 inches in diameter.

A live phalaenopsis plant from Java was sent in 1846 by Thomas Lobb to Veitch's Nursery and it bloomed in the collection of J. H. Schroeder, Esq. of Stratford Green. It was exhibited before the Royal Horticultural Society on September 7, 1847 and received a Silver Banksian Medal. Dr. Linley labeled it Phalaenopsis grandiflora, not recognizing it as Dr. Blume's Phalaenopsis amabilis.

PHALAENOPSIS STUARTIANA — Distinct from the amabilis group, P. stuartiana is endemic on Mindanao Island in the Philippines. The foliage is marbled on top, green and grey-green, and is purple underneath. The leaves are long and narrow and may reach 13 inches in length and be 3 inches wide. The variegations may fade out as the plant ages.

The flowers of Phal. stuartiana are small, about 2 1/2 inches wide, with dozens produced on a many-branched stem that may be two feet long. Herbert Shipman in Hilo has a plant of it that produced 544 flowers at once in 1933. The secret? He says he used to feed his phalaenopsis "Violet water, so called because it smelled so bad." The formula was one-half barley bag of chicken manure soaked in 50 gallons of water for at least a week, then diluted one quart to two gallons of water. The plants were watered, then fed with violet water, and the violet water then washed off the leaves.

The flowers of Phal. stuartiana are charming. They are white, distinguished by a suffusion of sulfur blotched with cinnamon on the inner half of the sepals and carried over onto the lip. It is used for breeding freckled phals.

Phal. stuartiana was discovered by a collector named Boxall in 1881 who was working for Stuart Low & Co. of London. The name honors Mr. Low.

White Hybrids

As hobby growers we do not have to make decisions about which phalaenopsis are species and which are merely varieties of that species. The taxonomists do this for us. But in following the current decision of the International Registration Authority, which lumps together as Phal. amabilis those previously listed under other names, it turns out that many of the big white hybrids of today are merely crossings of various strains of Phal. amabilis.

On a gold pedestal make a permanent design of camellia foliage treated with glycerine and dried wisteria stems. Hide flower tubes in the foliage and add fresh blooms. Arrangement by Ruby Mack.

But it could never be untangled. The thing to understand is that by whatever names these plants were registered, they represent selective breeding of flowers with desirable qualities. The result is to bring us through several generations to today's magnificent and apparently perfect white phalaenopsis flowers.

For instance, the good whites began with Phalaenopsis Elisabethae, registered from France in 1927 as Phal. amabilis x Phal. rimestadiana. Maurice Lecoufle told me that this Phal. rimestadiana was a plant they called "the white of Regnier," a fine variety discovered by Regnier (see more about him in the next chapter on pinks). Elisabethae is in the background of many of today's fine whites including Doris and remains in the hybrid lists as Elisabethae even though Phal. rimestadiana is now considered a variety of Phal. amabilis.

Likewise, Phalaenopsis Gilles Gratiot (Phal. aphrodite x Phal. rimestadiana) is actually now Phal. amabilis x Phal. amabilis and so the next generation, Phalaenopsis Katherine Siegwart (Phal. amabilis x Phal. Gilles Gratiot) is still only Phal. amabilis.

What happened with Katherine Siegwart, registered in 1932, was that crosses were made with selected parents in an effort to obtain a pure white phalaenopsis flower without the usual trace of pink or lavender on the back of the flower. It did just that. Then the best seedlings of the lot were crossed to improve the size and texture.

The early phalaenopsis were thin and wilted quickly. With succeeding generations inheriting Phal. rimestadiana's heavier than usual substance and the development of polyploids, it finally got so flowers could be cut and shipped. Now the whites have been improved to such a degree of durability that a cut spray of Phalaenopsis Bridesmaid 'Purity' was shipped from California to Australia and there declared Grand Champion of the Sixth World Orchid Conference Show in 1969.

Now we know that the fine early crosses were polyploids, but little was known about chromosomes at that time so it was hit or miss. (For more about chromosomes see YOU CAN GROW ORCHIDS and YOU CAN GROW CATTLEYA ORCHIDS).

The real milestone in breeding white phalaenopsis was Phalaenopsis Doris (Elisabethae x Katherine Siegwart) introduced by Duke Farms in 1940 and named for Doris Duke. Doris led other white phals for a while as a parent (145 offspring through 1970) and in getting awards (24 from AOS through 1970).

See Chapter V for the story of the pink Doris.

The first hybrid with Doris was Karen (Doris x Katherine Siegwart) registered in 1927 from Florida, followed in 1954 by Doris crossed with its other parent, Elisabethae, to make Martha. My plant of Martha blooms almost constantly with new spikes, secondary spikes and tertiary spikes branching off the secondary spikes. I grow it in a basket along with two if its keikis and often have six spikes at once. The flowers are medium sized and durable.

Doris struck paydirt with Grace Palm (Doris x Winged Victory), registered in 1950. Grace Palm has 27 AOS awards, the most to date and has been a parent 71 times so far. A fine stud is Juanita (Chief Tucker x Grace Palm).

Coming down the line, Chieftan, registered in 1949, is a stepping stone. It is Doris x La Canada. Then Cast Iron Monarch (1957) came along. It has Doris as a parent and as a grandparent and is a pentaploid. The plant has extremely thick large leaves and the flowers of heavy substance are carried on thick spikes. It is the parent of many famous white crosses including Mary Lou Stoddard and Joanna Magale.

In more recent generations of white we find these award-getters: Alice Gloria, Elinor Shaffer, Princess Grace, and Norman Peterson. Showing up frequently in the hybrid lists with these are Gertrude Beard, Wilma Hughes, and Susan Merkel, to mention a few.

Phalaenopsis Show Girl, white with red lip.

Phal. intermedia (above) and Phal. Sally Lowrey (left) are sources of red lips.

But it is interesting to note that while the advanced generations are being used for parents, the current registration lists frequently show Juanita, Grace Palm and Doris as parents.

Whites with Colored Lips

White cattleyas with colored lips have been around for some time, but white phalaenopsis with colored lips are newer and very exciting. In both genera these flowers may be designated as semi-alba or WCL (white-colored-lip.)

The phalaenopsis hybrids have glistening white sepals and petals and startling colored lips in varying shades of pink, rose, red, lavender and violet. Size and form are improving all the time.

The basic sources of the color are these species:

PHAL. EQUESTRIS (syn. Phal. rosea) is a Philippine species with one-inch blooms. It has white sepals and petals with rose shading at the center of the flower and on the column and dots on the ventral sepals. The lip is rust, rose-purple or violet.

PHAL. LINDENII has a lip with a heart-shaped mid-lobe lined with pink or purple. It is used in candy-stripe breeding, which see.

PHAL. VIOLACEA and PHAL. LUEDDEMANNIANA, described in Chapter VII, also contribute to colored lips, some lavender and violet.

PHAL. INTERMEDIA, a natural hybrid between Phal. equestris and Phal. aphrodite (amabilis) has small flowers with white tepals and rosy lips. The cross has been remade many times in cultivation.

Phal. intermedia var. portei has flowers larger than a typical Phal. intermedia, purple stains at the base of the white tepals, and the front lobe of the lip amethyst purple toned with red. Two plants of this variety were brought to England from the Philippines in 1861 by a French trader named Porte. In something of a record for floriferousness, at the Royal Horticultural Society on Dec. 17, 1912, a Lindley Medal was awarded to Lord Rothschild for a plant of Phal. intermedia var. portei that had been in his collection 30 years. It had three branched spikes with a total of 185 flowers, the largest spike having 13 branches with 84 flowers!

After a remake of Phal. intermedia, the first manmade hybrid with rosy lip color was Artemis (Phal. amabilis x Phal. rosea — now Phal. equestris) registered by Veitch in 1892. But there the development of semi-alba phals ceased until the Hawaiian growers went to work in the 1940's and produced Colin Potter (Elisabethae x Phal. intermedia var. portei) and Roselle (Elisabethae x Phal. equestris). Roselle and Doris gave us Ruby Lips. Mrs. Lester McCoy of Honolulu who made this cross told me that of the first batch of seedlings in 1955 about half of them had the desired lip color because of the dominance of the large white.

The important step came with Sally Lowrey, produced in Hawaii in 1953 (Pua Kea x Phal. equestris). Pua Kea is the second generation from Phal. amabilis and Phal. sanderiana, large white and pink species.

Sally Lowrey was used with large whites to increase flower size with colored lips in such hybrids as Judy Karleen (Sally Lowrey x Chieftan), Cover Girl (Sally Lowrey x Doris), and New Era (Sally Lowrey x Grace Palm). In later generations with this same line of breeding the results came out with about 25 percent really red lips, 50 percent colored lips ranging from lavender to coral, and 25 percent white. Some of the advanced red lips descended from this line are Carolyn Grandy, Karleen Tucker, Mad Hatter, Mad Lips, Rosy Mildred, Fiery, Dorleen and Cher Ann.

From the Phal. lueddemanniana line came Lipstick (Palm Beach x Star of Rio), then Show Girl (Doris x Lipstick), and so on.

A departure which produced some flowers with sparkling white tepals and dark cherry lips is Vandaenopsis Mem. Mari de Costa (Vanda cristata x Phal. Dos Pueblos). Vanda cristata has two-inch flowers of lime green with cherry red lips lined with white.

Cut a spray of Phalaenopsis Mambo and insert in a tube of water hidden behind a driftwood slab for an instant flower arrangement. Design by Ruby Mack.

Combine pink phalaenopsis with blue clipped sago in a handmade black wooden container for a handsome arrangement. The flowers are Phal. Zada and Phal. Mistinguett. Design by Ruby Mack.

CHAPTER V

PINK PHALAENOPSIS

The pink phalaenopsis have been developed into flowers of heavy substance, beautiful color in shades from the palest pastel to strawberry, in sizes from small to large. Some are striped like peppermint sticks.

PHALAENOPSIS SCHILLERIANA — In the Philippines the natives call Phal. schilleriana "tigre" because of the mottled grey and green foliage. Leaves are purple underneath and may grow to 20 inches in length. The roots are flat and rough.

The flowers measure 3 inches or more and bloom in the spring in great numbers on loosely branched spikes that may be 4 feet in length. The flowers are all open at the same time. They are fragrant in the morning until about 11 o'clock.

The flowers are soft pinkish-purple and the color fades to white at the outer edges. The inner half of the lateral sepals is dotted with reddish purple spots. The lip varies from almost white to deep magenta with dots on a yellow background on the inner portion of the lateral lobes. The flowers are charming but have little substance or durability. There are a number of recognized varieties.

It was named for Consul Schiller, a florist of Hamburg, Germany, who introduced it to Europe in 1858 and flowered it in 1860.

PHALAENOPSIS SANDERIANA — Similar to Phal. amabilis, Phal. sanderiana has been considered a variety of Phal. amabilis or Phal. aphrodite. It, too, is limited in distribution to the Philippines and a few adjacent islands.

The flowers vary in color from near white to deep rose-purple, the lip white with some yellow color and reddish or purplish stripes. They are not as large as the blooms of Phal. amabilis.

The foliage is dark green, sometimes with a brownish-purple suffusion on top and silver beneath.

Mr. Sander, for whom it is named, sent his collector, Roebbelen, to the Philippines in 1888 to look for a red phalaenopsis.

The search was not easy, as the natives in southern Mindanao, where the trail led, were unfriendly cannibals and only Roebbelen's association with a Chinese trader named Sam Choon saved his life and fulfilled his mission. He first saw the "red" phalaenopsis flowers in the coiffures of savages who bleached their hair and dyed it yellow and inserted brightly colored bird feathers, shells and flowers into their kinky yellow locks.

These two species, Phal. schilleriana and Phal. sanderiana, have been used in developing large pink phalaenopsis. Introduction of the large whites improved the substance but usually diluted the color. However, some of the early and famous pinks were quite beautiful.

Reve Rose was the beginning of the good pinks. A Frenchman named Regnier went to the South Pacific before World War I and brought back some fine varieties of Phal. schilleriana, Phal. amabilis and Phal. lueddemanniana. Reve Rose was Regnier's Phal. schilleriana crossed with Alger (Phal. aphrodite x Phal. sanderiana). Reve Rose was registered from France in 1932, and is a parent in succeeding generations of Pink Cloud, San Songer, Virginia, Rosada and Pink Sunset, to name a few of its progeny. It is a grandparent of Alice Bowen and Zada, and four times in the ancestry of some of the advanced hybrids such as Ann Marie Beard.

Marmouset, also descended from Regnier's species, is Ninon and Phal. schilleriana, a vigorous third generation hybrid with Phal. aphrodite once, and Phal. sanderiana and Phal. schilleriana each twice in its ancestry. In turn, Marmouset is a parent of such important hybrids as Aalsmeer Rose and Clara I. Knight and twice a grandparent of Clara Birk (Clara I. Knight x Aalsmeer Rose). Marmouset was registered in 1943.

Then came Mistinguett (Rothomogo x Helle) in 1956.

But the flower that was the breakthrough to durable pink phalaenopsis of size and quality was not a pink but a white.

Phalaenopsis Doris was selfed by the grower at Duke Farms and seedlings in flasks sold to a grower in South Florida. Some of these selfed

Phal. Zada x Phal. Zada.

whites reverted to a characteristic of Phal. amabilis by showing pink color on the back of the flowers and some of them even had a pink flush around the column. When the ones that showed the most pink were selfed and crossed, the inbreeding (now into the fifth generation) produced flowers where the pink genes became dominant and the pink color evenly spread front and back. This is called "pink Doris" but in the hybrid lists it is merely Doris.

A first generation tetraploid pink Doris was used as a parent with Marmouset to produce Clara I. Knight, registered in 1951. This was a milestone, as Clara I. Knight was the first pink phalaenopsis to win an American Orchid Society Award for quality. This was at the Miami show in February 1954, whereas white phalaenopsis had been getting quality awards since 1934. It was not until Alice Bowen began getting awards in 1958 that Clara I. Knight had any competition in the pink range, and to date Clara I. Knight has 10 AOS awards and Alice Bowen seven and

Phal. Ruby Lips, candy striped.

Elisa has 10. But note that the white Doris has 24 and Elinor Shaffer 17 awards to date.

A second generation pink Doris was used with San Songer (Reve Rose x Marmouset) to make Zada, flowered in Miami in 1958 and a really sensational pink phalaenopsis. Sibling crosses and selfings of Zada have produced additional fine pinks. P. Zadian (Zada x Phal. lueddemanniana) won an FCC/AOS in 1969 for 4-inch rose flowers of excellent form.

Others of Zada's descendants include Denise Richardson (Doris x Zada), Barbara Beard (Virginia x Zada) and Malibu Pink (Ann Lovelace x Zada).

Alice Bowen (Dark Hawaii x Pink Cloud), registered from Honolulu in 1955, is a bright pink of rather star-shaped design derived from six parts Phal. schilleriana and three parts Phal. amabilis with a dash of Phal. sanderiana, Phal. lueddemanniana and Phal. stuartiana.

This line began with Phal. Regnier made by Regnier with his Phal. lueddemanniana x Phal. schilleriana and registered in 1922. The flower has open form but deep pink color from minute dots all over the surface.

The next generation gave Dark Hawaii (Hawaii x Regnier), a 2-inch ruby flower with open shape.

Aalsmeer Rose, registered in 1960, is Ruby x Marmouset and goes back to both pink and white species. Crossed with Grace Palm it is a parent of Elisa, a large pink with size and shape comparable to the whites, and of Roswell, a vivacious bright pink flower.

There's no doubt the pinks have arrived.

Another line that is improving the pinks is the addition of yellow, which sometimes intensifies the pink. The intergeneric pinks are discussed in a later chapter.

Candy Stripes

PHALAENOPSIS LINDENII — This is a charming little flower, whitish or slightly pinkish, with some radiating stripes on the teardrop lip. It has faint stripes in the sepals and petals and it breeds candy-striped flowers. The stripes seem to be minute dots closely placed in a pattern. Phal.

Phal. Wanda Williams. A primary hybrid (Phal. lindenii x Phal. amboinensis), it has rosy orchid stripes on white segments.

lindenii grows in the mountains of Luzon at 5,000 feet in areas with lots of moisture.

Baguio (Phal. lindenii x Phal. schilleriana) generally blooms with obvious stripes but the size factor from Phal. lindenii is dominant as even the awarded ones are less than 2 inches natural spread. Peppermint (Phal. lindenii x Pink Profusion) also comes with stripes.

Phal. Jimmy Arnold (Ruby Lips x Rosada) has pink stripes and a dark pink lip.

PHALAENOPSIS LUEDDEMANNIANA — Some striping derives from Phal. lueddemanniana, notably in the line from Show Girl, a white with red lip. Some Show Girls have stripes and some breed it as in Ella Freed (Show Girl x Samba). Renee Freed (Show Girl x Phal. violacea) got a FCC/AOS on its first bloom, which was purple with dark amethyst striations radiating from the center of the flower. Natural spread of this bloom was 2¼ inches.

Rosy Charm (Hermoine x Pink Wave) registered in 1962, is a stepping stone. It goes back to Phal. lueddemanniana and Phal. stuartiana. Rosy Charm has 3-inch flowers with heavy spotting and has 12 awards to date, the most of the pink phals.

Ministripes (Pinocchio x Rosy Charm), made with parents having polyploid characteristics but no stripes, has produced some good striped flowers. It has Phal. equestris, Phal. lueddemanniana and Phal. schilleriana in its ancestry.

PHALAENOPSIS EQUESTRIS (syn. Phal. rosea) — This is another source of stripes, notably through Roselle (Elisabethae x Phal. equestris) and Ruby Lips (Roselle x Doris). Some of the awarded Ruby Lips have attractive rose or lavender stripes. One awarded Jimmy Arnold (Ruby Lips x Rosada) bloomed with pink flowers striped with darker pink on the tepals and with dark pink lips. An awarded Jack McQuerry (Suemid x Ruby Lips) is striped with heliotrope and the gold lip is striped with lavender. Candy Wakasugi (Texas Star x Ruby Lips) has been awarded for attractive striped flowers.

Continued selective breeding is expected to provide even finer striped flowers, and perhaps, when crossed with large whites, to increase the flower size.

Natural hybrids. (Left) Phal leucorrhoda = Phal aphrodite (amabilis) x Phal. schilleriana. (Below) Phal. veitchiana = Phal. schilleriana x Phal. rosea (equestris).

CHAPTER VI

YELLOW PHALAENOPSIS

The search for yellow in phalaenopsis is a recent trend, for while there are several species with yellow color, their flowers are small by comparison with the whites and pinks. The idea of producing yellow phalaenopsis did not catch the fancy of the hybridizers, except for a few early tries, until a few years ago. Lost time is being made up as many growers try for sunshine yellow flowers of good size and shape.

Yellow Species

Let's take a look at the species that are a source of yellow.

PHALAENOPSIS MANNII (Syn. Phal. boxallii) — This species comes from Sikkim, Assam and Vietnam, generally higher and cooler locations than other species. The plants are small, the leaves about a foot long at the most. The inflorescences are short and sometimes branched with a dozen or less flowers that are about 1½ inches across and 2 inches long.

The shellacked sepals and petals are golden yellow or yellow-green. They are barred longitudinally and also horizontally on the inner halves of the lateral sepals with rich chestnut brown. The segments are narrow and pointed with the petals smaller than the sepals in both width and length. The edges of the segments tend to curve backward. The flower appears bowlegged like a cowboy.

The side lobes of the lip are light yellow, the middle lobe slightly fringed, white, and shaped like an anchor. The naked column is gold at the front and red at the base.

PHALAENOPSIS LUEDDEMANNIANA — Some varieties of this species are yellow.

Phal. lueddemanniana var. ochracea is the same size and shape as the typical amethyst-purple type of Phal. lueddemanniana. It has a ground color of white to cream. The bars are reddish-brown to ochre and vary from plant to plant in width and intensity of color. The midlobe of the lip is amethyst which runs over onto the bases of the sepals and petals.

Phal. lueddemanniana var. pallens (syn. Phal. pallens) has flowers varying from corn yellow and light lemon to greenish. The cinnamon markings are delicately traced in transverse lines and dashes. The lip is white.

There is considerable confusion about the identity as plants in cultivation may have either name. In the past it was known as Trichoglottis pallens and Phal. foerstermannii.

PHALAENOPSIS SUMATRANA — Obviously discovered in Sumatra, this species was reported by Korthals prior to 1839. It grows in the shade on trees over or near water along with Phal. violacea. It is also indigenous to Java, Borneo, the Mentawei Islands, Malaya, Perak, Johore and Thailand.

The 2-inch flowers are off-white or lemon-yellow and sometimes tinged with green. The tepals have transverse cinnamon stripes and the lip is lightly lined with two magenta stripes.

PHALAENOPSIS MARIAE — It may belong in the yellows, as it has segments that are white or cream and marked with heavy blotches of maroon or chestnut brown. The lip is pale mauve. It was found on Sulu, a small island between the Philippines and Borneo, later found in these countries also.

PHALAENOPSIS CORNU-CERVI — It has small pointed flowers of mustard yellow or yellowish-green. The cinnamon brown blotches and bars are concentrated in the narrow petals, the dorsal sepal and the outer halves of the lateral sepals.

The inflorescence, which remains green after the flowers have wilted and which continues to bloom over a long period, is flat and zigzagged.

Phalaenopsis Helen Kuhn (Phal. Zada x Phal. fuscata).

This characteristic gives the species its name, which translates "stag's horn."

According to the accounts of an early collector reported in Veitch's Manual, Phal. cornu-cervi was found growing in dense shade on mango trees in Burma where it was evergreen, but where it grew along the mouth of the Irrawaddy River exposed to the sun it was deciduous, its roots kept plump during the dormant season by nocturnal dews. Phal. cornu-cervi is native to a large area from Java into Burma.

A natural hybrid between Phal. cornu-cervi and Phal. violacea, reported in 1883, is Phal. valentini with purple sepals and petals and some purple bands and said to have obvious characteristics of both parents.

PHALAENOPSIS FUSCATA — This flower has a different pattern —no spots or bars but large splotches of chocolate brown on the inner portions of the yellow sepals and petals and repeated on the lip. It is found in the Philippines and was introduced in 1897. It is one of the last of the yellows to be used for hybridizing as its first hybrid, Janet Kuhn, was registered from Florida in 1965. It apparently transmits excellent color.

PHALAENOPSIS FASCIATA (syn. Phal. reichenbachiana) — This one has a ground color of light to deep yellow, sometimes greenish. It is marked with reddish-brown transverse bars. The lateral lobes of the lip are yellow dotted with red and the midlobe vivid orange at the base and magenta at the apex. It was introduced in 1882 from the Philippines.

PHALAENOPSIS COCHLEARIS — This species is new, being reported by Dr. R. E. Holttum in 1964. It comes from Sarawak and has pale yellow-green flowers with a couple of brown bars on each segment near the column.

The distinctive lip is spoon-shaped with eight red-brown lines radiating from the base to the edges. The inflorescence may be 12 inches long, but usually has only two flowers open at once.

The hybrid of Phal. cochlearis x Golden Sands is yellow with brown spots.

PHALAENOPSIS CORNINGIANA — It comes from Malaya, is pale greenish with lengthwise bars of cinnamon. The midlobe of the lip and the base of the column are bright magenta, the side lobe and the column are white. It was named in 1879 by Reichenbach for a pioneer orchid hobbyist, Erastus Corning of Albany, N.Y., but it has either been unavailable or just not appreciated for cultivation or hybridizing until recently.

PHALAENOPSIS MICHOLITZII is extremely rare. It comes from the southern islands of the Philippines. It has a flower of cream to pale yellow or green, about 2½ inches across. The blooms open one at a time on a short spike.

Yellow Hybrids

Veitch registered a hybrid of two species in 1898 as Stuartianomannii, and Hymen (Phal. lueddemanniana x Phal. mannii) in 1900. This latter has small open flowers barred with reddish-brown.

Phalaenopsis Golden Chief (Phal. Chieftan x Phal. mannii).

Then Atherton in Hawaii flowered Sumabilis (Phal. sumatrana x Phal amabilis) in 1938 which had small yellow flowers.

There it ended until the 1950's with the arrival of Mannipam, Golden Louis, Golden Chief, Valentine's Day, Moonglow and other early yellows.

Golden Louis (Doris x Phal. mannii) was registered in 1957 from Florida. The first flower was honey gold without the Phal. mannii barring, a size and shape between that of the two parents, and good substance. It had a suffusion of soft rose color around the column and flowers of 3 to 3½ inches in width, the lip yellow marked with red. A good proportion of the seedlings were yellow.

This was the breakthrough, followed by Golden Chief (Chieftan and Phal. mannii) in 1958, generally with better shape.

Golden Palm (Grace Palm x Phal. mannii) registered from California in 1959 and Gold Coast (Hymen x Doris) both gave a fair percentage of yellow flowers. Some of them fade out in the light as they mature.

A cross flowered about 1950 named Mannipam (Phal. mannii x Pamela) was not registered.

Valentine's Day (Hymen x P. amabilis var. grandiflora) was registered in 1958. A few were yellow.

Golden Martha (Joanna Magale x Phal. mannii), 1962, produced some good clones of high ploidy, but some were aneuploids.

Golden Sands, which was registered from Florida in 1964, is a consistent award winner. It is Fenton Davis Avant (a big white) x Phal. lueddemanniana var. ochracea. The ground color is bright yellow, the spotting bright but not overwhelming, and the form excellent in many clones. Thirteen clones were awarded in the first four years with the one that received a FCC/AOS named 'Canary.' Most of them are recorded as butter yellow to lime yellow with overall spotting of rose with tangerine lips. The size is slightly under 4 inches.

Moonglow (Phal. sumatrana x Springtime) was registered from Florida in 1958. It is creamy, spotted with red, and is generally triploid. Moonclurie (Moonglow x Palm Beach) is pastel yellow-green with a lavender flush at the center.

But put Phal. sumatrana with Dos Pueblos (a big white) and this makes Ruth Wallbrunn which is cream, spotted all over with lavender pinpoint dots and a yellow lip marked with orange. Carrousel, a dark Phal. sumatrana with a big white (Katherine Pillsbury) is similar.

The crosses made with Phal. fuscata have produced some striking spotted flowers. Janet Kuhn (Phal. fuscata x Dos Pueblos) has enchanting blooms of varying shades of yellow vividly marked with purple or magenta spots arranged in lines, and bright orange lips. Some hybrids of Phal. fuscata and big whites are solid yellow.

The combination of yellow and pink phalaenopsis has produced some delightful colors from salmon to bronze.

Little Brown Gal (Sunrise x Phal. mannii) from Hawaii in 1964 is well named. So are Amber Sky (Phal. mannii x Radiant Glow) and Sandalwood (Gold Coast x Phal. sanderiana.)

So, the yellows have progressed dramatically in a few years and will improve as time goes on.

An easier way, however, seems to be in intergeneric hybridizing. The yellow color is dominant in the renantheras, and this might be an easier route to yellow than the one that has been taken with the small-flowered phalaenopsis. See chapter on Multigenerics.

CHAPTER VII

NOVELTIES

Phalaenopsis lueddemanniana

Phalaenopsis lueddemanniana has a 2-inch flower of heavy substance shaped rather like a fat star. It comes in a variety of colors although it is basically magenta on white or brown on yellow. The segments are barred with the darker color and some of the flowers are overlaid with a dark reddish tone. The back of the flower is white. The lip is bright carmine touched with yellow, the column is purple.

The leaves are light green, narrow, up to 9 inches long. The scapes are fine and flexible and reach out about a foot. Many flowers appear at the ends of the stems over a long period.

All this may not seem very exciting, but don't let "luedde" fool you.

Just before the turn of this century, five hybrids were made with Phal. lueddemanniana. Another appeared in 1922, but about 1950 when another batch began blooming, things started popping. Since that time, Phal. lueddemanniana has figured greatly in the development of new phalaenopsis, as already obvious from previous chapters.

Phal. lueddemanniana is native to the Philippines. It was introduced into Europe in 1864 and named for Monsieur Lueddemann of Paris who flowered it in 1865. The Royal Horticultural Society gave it a First Class Certificate (F.C.C.) that year.

The five original crosses were made at Veitch's nursery:

x Phal. amabilis = John Seden, 1888
x Phal. stuartiana = Hermoine, 1899
x Phal. mannii = Hymen, 1900
x Phal. violacea = Luedde-violacea, 1895
x Phal. sanderiana = Mrs. J. H. Veitch (syn. Luzon), no date.

Next came Phal. Regnier (Phal. lueddemanniana x Phal. schilleriana), in 1922, then three crosses registered in 1949-50.

The breakthrough was the tenth hybrid when Phal. lueddemanniana was crossed with a tetraploid Doris (what else?) and Nuel N. Songer was registered from Florida in 1952. The flowers have great variability depending on the "luedde" used, but some are star shaped ivory flowers dotted all over with bright amethyst purple and with lips from blush to purple. Some flowers have no spots at all, but all have heavy substance and long lasting blooms, maybe two months. Flower size is from 2 inches to 4½, depending on the dominance of the big or little parent.

There followed a long line of stars made in Europe and the U. S. having the star shape, heavy substance and varying degrees of spotting and color intensity. When the parent "luedde" has light bars the progeny have light flowers with a minimum of spotting. When it has dark bars the color and density of the spotting are generally greater. Alice Bowen, for example, was made with a dark red Phal. lueddemanniana ancestor, and the intense spotting carries over into succeeding generations, as witness Alice Bowen x Zada, a fifth generation away from the original Phal. lueddemanniana, but still with brilliant spots.

As to durability, I once wore a flower of Star of Santa Cruz every day for a week after it had crossed a continent and an ocean.

Many of the Phal. lueddemanniana hybrids have been used extensively as parents: Hymen x Dos Pueblos = Masu Hamacher; Hymen x Gloriosa = Sunset Glow; Mrs. J. H. Veitch x Juanita = Painted Desert; Texas Star x Susan Merkel = Key Lime.

A much-awarded starry phalaenopsis is Inspiration (Phal. lueddemanniana x Juanita), registered from California in 1961 with flowers generally 3½ inches wide, with touching tepals, ranging from chartreuse to lemon with scattered pink to reddish spots and brightly colored lips.

Phal. Hymen hybrids. (Top) x Phal. Gloriosa = Sunset Glow, garnet color. (Left) x Phal. amboinensis = Hi Boy, copper. (Right) x Phal. Louis Merkel = Hylo, white with raspberry spots.

One of its many offspring is Jacksonville Study (Inspiration x Mrs. J. H. Veitch), named for our Study Group.

Phal. lueddemanniana var. pulchra (synonym: Phal. pulchra or Phal. lueddemanniana var. purpurea) has waxy blooms up to 2 inches across of brilliant deep magenta-purple so solid that the typical striping of "luedde" is not obvious. It blooms all summer long and makes keikis so freely that you can soon fill a large pot or treefern basket with the offshoots of one plant. Merely curve the long stems to which they are attached into the container and peg plants down with hairpins.

The purple "luedde" contributes color to make lavender and magenta phalaenopsis.

Phalaenopsis violacea

Phalaenopsis violacea is producing some exciting hybrids. There are two forms of the species with different color patterns.

The Borneo form (also from Sumatra and Java) is cream shading to green margins, with a brilliant triangle of deep violet at the center of the flower from above the column down the inner half of the lateral sepals and on the lip. The Malaya form has the rose-magenta color suffused

Flowers on opposite page:
- A. **Phal. lueddemanniana var. pallens**
- B. **Phal micholitzii**
- C. **Phal. gigantea**
- D. **Phal. amabilis**
- E. **Phal. lueddemanniana var. pulchra**
- F. **Phal. fasciata**
- G. **Phal sanderiana**

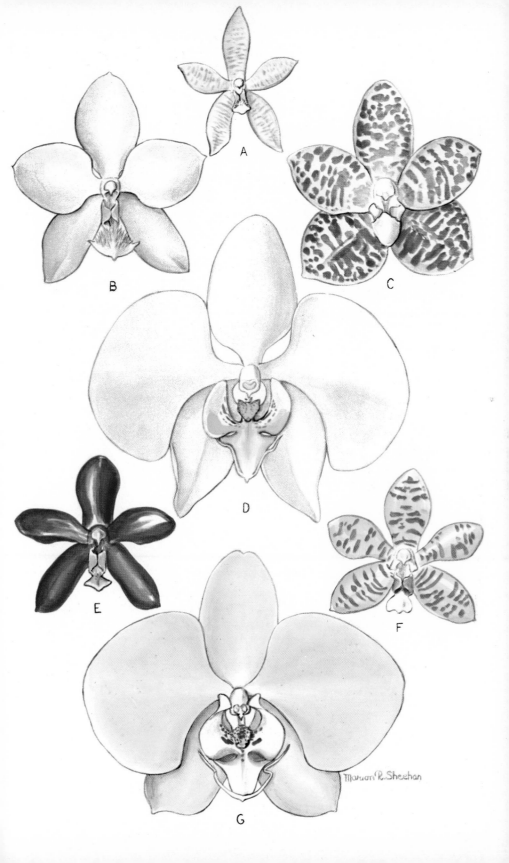

A

B

C

D

E

F

G

Marion R. Sheehan

Phalaenopsis Harriettiae, the first hybrid.

uniformly over the sepals and petals, which have greenish tips. It is not as bowlegged as the Borneo form.

There is a good deal of variation in the color intensity and the patterns within this species, and there is an albino form. The flowers run 2 to 3 inches wide, and the light green leaves 6 to 10 inches long and 3 to 4 inches wide. The Borneo form is a larger plant with larger flowers than its Malaya counterpart.

The plants grow in the lowlands on trees hanging over streams in hot, damp forests.

In 1887 Veitch registered the first Phalaenopsis hybrid, Phal. Harriettiae (named in honor of Erastus Corning's daughter, because Mr. Corning of Albany, N. Y. bought the only plant of the hybrid that was raised to maturity.) This plant is still in existence, along with some keikis. Phal. Harriettiae received a FCC/RHS in 1887 and an AM/AOS in 1958.

It has 3-inch flowers of cream stained with rose-purple on the basal half.

Phal. Ludde-violacea has been remade many times and produces lacquered star-shaped blooms of brilliant magenta, cerise, or red-purple.

Only a few more hybrids were made until the 1960's perhaps because the few plants in cultivation were the Borneo variety and it is difficult to breed.

Crosses with big whites give such hybrids as Therese Frakowiak, Beach Violet, Violita, Amethyst, and Malaysian Star. The polyploid whites tend to dilute the color but add size and better form. Phal. violacea imparts substance, texture and bright lip color, as well as strong tepal color if the other parent is a diploid. Many interesting crosses are being made with flowers of other colors, and with other genera:

x Phal. cochlearis = Little Darlin'
x Golden Chief = Raspberry Jam
x Pinocchio = Pink Elf.
x Dtps. Red Coral = Dtps. Violet

Flowers on next page:
A. **Phal. parishii**
B. **Doritis pulcherrima**
C. **Phal. equestris (rosea)**
D. **Phal. mannii**
E. **Phal. lindenii**
F. **Phal. mannii**
G. **Phal. schilleriana**
H. **Phal. lueddemanniana**
I. **Phal. Hymen (lueddemanniana x mannii)**
J. **Phal. fimbriata**
K. **Phal. stuartiana**

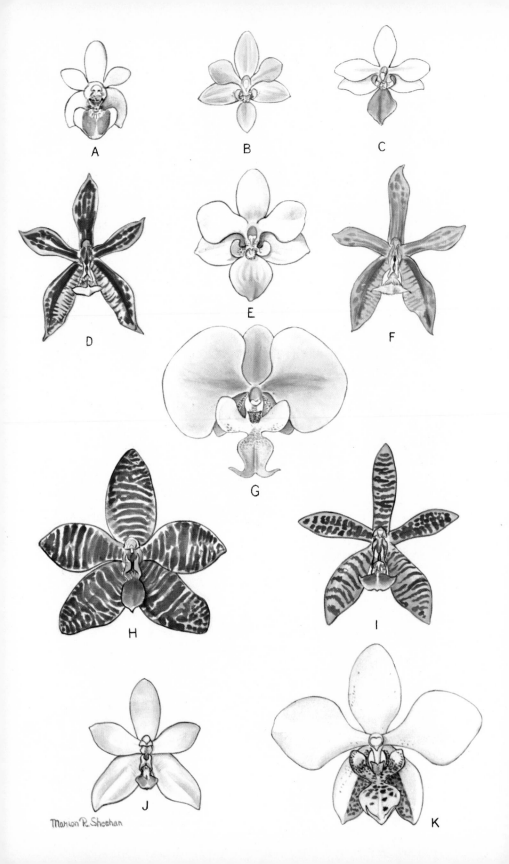

A

B

C

D

E

F

G

H

I

J

Marion R. Sheehan

K

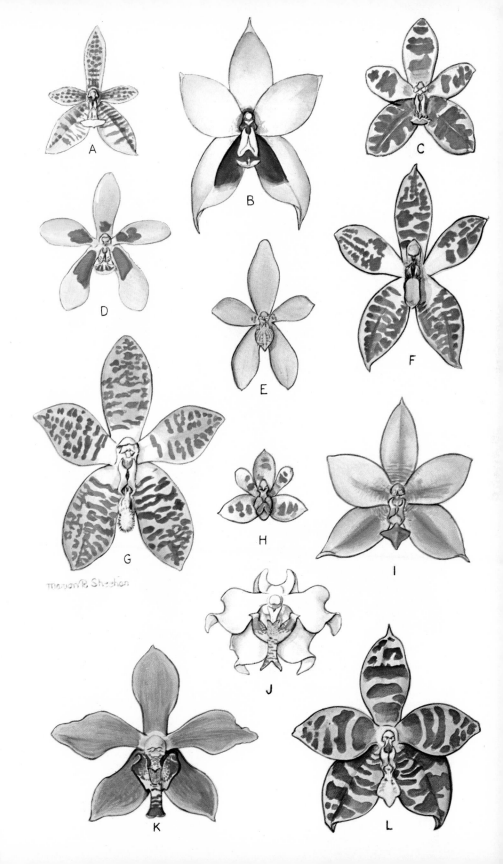

marian R. Sheehan

Flowers on preceding page:

    A. Phal. cornu-cervi
    B. Phal. violacea (Borneo)
    C. Phal. mariae
    D. Phal. fuscata
    E. Phal. cochlearis
    F. Phal. corningiana
    G. Phal. sumatrana
    H. Phal. maculata
    I. Phal. violacea (Malaya)
    J. Phal. serpentilingua
    K. Phal. denevei
    L. Phal. amboinensis

Phalaenopsis gigantea

Phalaenopsis gigantea gets its name not from the flowers but from the enormous leaves. These may be more than 2 feet long and a foot wide, whereas the flowers are only about 2 to 2½ inches across. There are many blooms all open at once on long pendulous racemes between drooping leaves.

The flower has wide segments which give it a rounded form. It looks cupped because it hangs down. The back is white, the front of the flower is basically white but covered all over with red-brown blotches. It has a white lip with crimson lines. The heavy substance of the bloom

Phal. gigantea hybrids. (Above) x Phal. Baguio = Phal. Janet
Ragan. (Below) x Phal. stuartiana = Phal. Gretchen.

Vandaenopsis Mari de Costa

Phalaenopsis Lois Jansen 'Gertie,' HCC/AOS

Phalaenopsis Carnival 'Malibu,' HCC/AOS

Phalaenopsis Amber Sands
'Gertie,' AM/AOS

Phalaenopsis cochlearis x Phalaenopsis Golden Sands

Beardara Charles Beard

is desirable in hybridizing, although the foliage size is transmitted to the offspring and big plants take space.

Phal. gigantea is native to Borneo where black bees gather its honey. Only one plant survived in cultivation from the original collection made in 1896-7. A new source of supply found in the 1930's has provided plants for selfing and crossing.

The first hybrid was Bogoriensis (Phal. gigantea x Phal. amabilis) registered in 1936 by the Botanical Garden of Bogor (formerly Buitenzorg) in Java. It has white blooms with brown spots.

The first of more recent hybrids is Mok Choi Yew (Phal. gigantea x Phal. violacea) registered in 1968 from Singapore. The flower is 2 x 2 inches, light greenish background with maroon spots. The midlobe of the lip and the column are clear yellow, the side lobes marked with maroon. It retains the fragrance of Phal. violacea.

Gretchen (Phal. gigantea x Phal. stuartiana) registered from Florida has 2½ inch flowers, which flushed yellow with vivid brown-lavender spots and a rust colored lip. It sometimes has 40 or 50 flowers on a spike.

Phal. gigantea x Samba has spots and looks like an improved Samba. Phal. gigantea x Baguio is named Janet Ragan, is cream with tiny red spots.

Phalaenopsis amboinensis

This species comes from the island of Amboina or Ambon and other islands in the Moluccas, which lie between New Guinea and Borneo.

It has heavy cinnamon bars on the sepals and petals, which are narrower on the inner halves of the lateral sepals. The base color of the flower is white, chartreuse or yellow, the tips of the segments greenish.

Some very interesting crosses are coming from Phal. amboinensis. Mambo (Phal. amboinensis x Phal. mannii) has much wider segments than Phal. mannii, with intense yellow and brown color and a white lip.

Samba (Star of Rio x Phal. amboinensis) has sensational flowers of extremely heavy substance and wide flat segments of ivory with amethyst circles radiating from the center. The column and lip are bright amethyst.

Wanda Williams (**Phal.** amboinensis x Phal. lindenii) comes with rosy stripes on white that run longitudinally on the segments.

Tuffy (Phal. amboinensis x Lowana Goldlip) has 3-inch cream flowers with amethyst spots and the excellent substance and texture of Phal. amboinensis.

Phalaenopsis parishii

A little gem among phalaenopsis is Phal. parishii var. lobbii which comes from the eastern Himalayas. This is a small plant with leaves only 3 to 4 inches long. The 1-inch flowers are produced on short stems close to the foliage. The flower is milky white with a crescent shaped lip with two wide brown vertical bands on it. It is hinged under the column and wiggles when the plant is touched.

The variety is the one generally in cultivation. Phal. parishii is found in Burma and has a magenta midlobe on the lip. It grows on moss-covered branches over water. Other plants that grow in positions exposed to drought are deciduous. Phal. parishii var. lobbii, when grown in cultivation, should not be deprived of water nor allowed to drop its foliage.

A few hybrids, some intergeneric, have been made.

(Left) Phal. parishii. (Below) Phal. Partris (Phal. parishii x Phal. equestris).

Phalaenopsis Louis Merkel 'Julie,' Bronze Medal, 5th World Orchid Conference.

Phalaenopsis Bridesmaid 'Purity,' Grand Champion, 6th World Orchid Conference.

Phalaenopsis Frances Roberts

Phalaenopsis Zada

Phalaenopsis maculata

Phal. maculata might belong under the pinks. It has a 1-inch flower with a cream-colored base and reddish-brown blotches. The lip is deep reddish-purple. Phal. maculata comes from Sarawak and Malaysia and flowered at Veitch's in 1881.

Phalaenopsis fimbriata

Phal. fimbriata is providing a route to green through its fleshy flower which is almost white or tinted pale green. It has a touch of amethyst on the lateral sepals beside the lip and an amethyst lip fringed with white.

CHAPTER VIII

TERETE PHALAENOPSIS

There are three species of Phalaenopsis that are unlike the rest of the genus because they have terete leaves. The Malayans call them "rat-tailed phals."

Terete means cylindrical, and the leaves are round and stiff like pencils with grooves in them. They are like the terete vandas except the phalaenopsis plants have more of a fan pattern with the leaves joining the stem at the base rather than in the more stair-step manner of the vandas. Terete phalaenopsis leaves may be 30 inches long, are dark bluish green.

These species, Phal. denevei, Phal. laycockii and Phal. serpentilingua are native to Borneo and Sarawak but have been ruthlessly collected and may be extinct in Sarawak.

PHAL. DENEVEI — The flowers of Phal. denevei are produced on a short scape with up to 12 in a rather close cluster near the base of the leaves. The sepals and petals are of equal size and the flower has a 2-inch spread.

The sepals and petals are yellowish-green overlaid with bronze, rather like a mustard and olive combination, sometimes chartreuse at the tips and around the edges. The lip varies from old rose to crimson. The column is white.

The plants grow on trees beside rivers and can stand strong sun if the air is humid. They bloom in the rainy season.

PHAL. SERPENTILINGUA — It is so named because the midlobe of the lip looks like the forked tongue of a snake. The flowers are

Phalaenopsis Ruth Wallbrunn 'Fort Caroline,' AM/AOS

Renanthopsis Ginger McQuerry

Phalaenopsis Spice Islands 'Ruth Wallbrunn,' AM/AOS

Ascovandoritis Sonnhild Kitts

Asconopsis Irene Dobkin 'Rayna,' AM/AOS

Doritaenopsis Lizanne Galbreath

white to light rose and the lip is barred red and yellow. The blooms are smaller and have less substance than those of Phal. denevei. The foliage is similar to Phal. denevei but the flowers are produced on longer stems.

PHAL. LAYCOCKII is elusive. It has been found twice and lost twice. The flowers are shaped like those of Phal. denevei, slightly larger and pale lavender with darker lips.

Phal. laycockii was first discovered in 1934 from the interior of South Borneo and one plant bloomed in Singapore for John Laycock in 1936. (It is named for him.) The plant died.

It was not seen again until 1961 when a "pink denevei" was produced by an Indonesian who smuggled it across the border into Sarawak. It was planted in Kuching, but alas, it died.

Recently a third Phal. laycockii turned up, and crosses with the other teretes have been made.

Terete Hybrids

A number of interesting hybrids have been made lately mostly in Singapore, Indonesia and Hawaii with the terete species.

Sunny is Phal. denevei x Phal. serpentilingua. Kolopaking is Phal. laycockii x Phal. serpentilingua, and has the forked lip of Phal. serpentilingua.

Apparently the Phal. denevei is very fertile. The Phal. serpentilingua hybrids seem to pick up the colors from the other parent.

Most of the hybrids have been made with Arachnis, which makes Arachnopsis, or Vanda, making Vandaenopsis. Cross Arachnopsis x Vanda and the genus is Trevorara.

To pick a few:

Arachnopsis Eric Holttum (Arachnis Maggie Oei x Phal. denevei). Arachnopsis Napier (Arachnopsis Eric Holttum x Phal. denevei). Arachnopsis Nirmala (Arachnis Ishbel x Phal. serpentilingua).

Vandaenopsis Patience (Phal. denevei x Vanda Rothschildiana) has 2½ inch flowers of cobalt violet with darker veins. The segments are wider than Phal. denevei but not wide enough to imitate the closed form

Vandaenopsis Serpentinda (Phalaenopsis serpentilingua x Vanda teres). White tepals, apricot lip
with red striations.

of a good Roth. Vandaenopsis Sophie (Phal. serpentilingua x Vanda
Rothschildiana) is a miniature with flowers from reddish-pink to light
blue.

Vandaenopsis Prosperitas (Vanda dearei x Phal. denevei) looks like
a miniature Vanda dearei with some flowers clear yellow, others faintly
marked, and a lip marked with red-brown.

Aeridopsis Trengganu (Phal. serpentilingua x Aerides odorata) has a
pleasing fragrance though not as pungent as the Aer. odorata parent.
The semi-pendulous stem carries two dozen or more flowers, each an
inch or more in diameter, ivory white with a faint pink overlay, the lip
deep rose with darker striations, the spur greenish white. The semi-
terete leaves grow upright, and the roots are heavy like those of aerides.

For other hybrids, see Chapter X, Multigenerics.

CHAPTER IX

RELATED GENERA

Doritis

Doritis pulcherrima is a close relative of Phalaenopsis and many beautiful hybrids have been made by combining these genera as Doritaenopsis.

DORITIS PULCHERRIMA is a small-flowered species that has blooms about an inch wide strung along slender spikes. They begin to open at the bottom of the upright spike, one flower at a time a few days apart. If the spike keeps elongating, as it is prone to do, it begins to arch with its own length. Flowers continue to open at the top and the old ones at the bottom gradually fall off. A plant may be in bloom for months.

The little flowers show much variation in size, color intensity and pattern. They run from white through pale pink to bright magenta.

The bloom has a pointed lip and the petals and the sepals tend to reflex in varying degrees. The name is from the Greek "doru" meaning spear or lance in reference to the spear-shaped lip. The lip is always darker than the tepals.

Dor. pulcherrima, called "mah-wing" or "running horse" in Thai has attractive foliage. There are several pairs of leaves stacked one above the other but closely spaced on the stem, making it a taller and leafier plant than the general run of phalaenopsis plants. But the foliage is not as succulent nor as glossy as phalaenopsis foliage, nor is it as wide.

This plant grows all over Thailand, also in Indochina, Burma, Malaysia and Sumatra. It is not particular about its habitat as in Thailand and Malaysia it grows in sandy soil in the shade of shrubs in the mountains or in forests rooted in leafmold between stones, or on rocks near the sea.

The rainy season lasts from May until October in some sections of its habitat, and winter from November to February. It is very dry in the cool months and the plants may shrivel and shed their leaves. In another area of its habitat the rain falls for 10 months of the year.

The recognized names now are Doritis pulcherrima for the diploid* or smaller form and Doritis pulcherrima var. buyssoniana for the tetraploid* form with larger flowers.

DORITIS PULCHERRIMA VAR. BUYSSONIANA has larger flowers than the other and they are not so inclined to reflex. The Thai name is "Daeng Ubol," the first word means red and Ubol is its habitat near the Mekong River. The tetraploid and diploid forms do not grow in the same places.

Var. buyssoniana grows where the winter is cool and dry for four months and it lives among small grasses in open terrain with its roots in black soil derived from limestone. It may shed its leaves in March or April but when the rainy season begins it grows and flowers.

The flowers of the variety show extensive variation in size, color and form and are about twice the size (around 2 inches) of the diploid blooms and stand up nice and flat. The color is from almost white and light lavender to dark magenta, but the dark ones are not as dark as the darkest diploids.

The foliage of var. buyssoniana is larger and thicker and more leathery than that of Dor. pulcherrima. Sometimes the leaves are suffused or spotted with purple.

In cultivation, doritis plants grow with phalaenopsis, needing good drainage. Any combination of organic materials such as crushed rock, tree fern, bark or other mixtures serve for potting. Liberal watering year round will keep the plants succulent and prevent leaf drop.

---

* For explanation of these terms and chromosomes, see YOU CAN GROW CATTLEYA ORCHIDS, the chapter called "Chromosomes Count."

Doritis pulcherrima var. buyssoniana 'Marshall,' HCC/AOS

These plants grow into clumps by producing keikis, and if grown in large containers the keikis can be left in place. A colony is attractive in a large flat treefern basket and makes a good show when in bloom.

There has been a lot of name switching during the years, and Phalaenopsis esmeralda was the choice for a long time. But in 1958 the name of Doritis pulcherrima was returned, and previous hybrids listed with Phal. esmeralda changed. Another synonym is Phal. antennifera.

Doritis Hybrids

Doritis pulcherrima really shines as a parent with phalaenopsis to make Doritaenopsis (Dtps.)

The hybrids tend to have long upright or arching spikes with the blooms nicely spaced, and to flower over a long period.

The flower size is generally between that of the parents. In advanced generations blooms equal phalaenopsis hybrids in size. The substance of the flowers is good, generally heavier than straight phalaenopsis crosses.

The doritis seems to be dominant for color when used with phalaenopsis. However, using a small doritis with a large white phalaenopsis dilutes the color. And unfortunately, in many doritaenopsis the bright color fades out at the edges of the tepals.

Crossing Dor. pulcherrima with phalaenopsis eliminates the reflexing habit and results in nice flat flowers. This combination also results in a phalaenopsis-shaped lip with short antennae. When var. buyssoniana is used, the color may be brighter and the doritis shape is more pronounced.

The first cross was Doritaenopsis Asahi (Dor. pulcherrima x Phal. lindenii) registered from Hawaii in 1923. Nothing else happened until the 1950's when six hybrids were registered. The milestone that caught attention was Dtps. Red Coral (Dor. pulcherrima x Phal. Doris.) The Doris was a pink one, and the cross made in Wisconsin.

Red Coral has the most doritaenopsis awards to date, and probably has been used as a parent more than any others. Some of its progeny include:

x Phal. Zada = Dtps. Clarelen

x Phal. violacea = Dtps. Violet

x Phal. Therese Frackowiak = Dtps. Jerry Vande Weghe

x Dor. pulcherrima = Dtps. Fire Cracker.

An awarded Red Coral is described with 63 flowers and 45 buds on two spikes, each flower 2¾ inches natural spread, rose pink in color.

Doritaenopsis Mem. Clarence Schubert (Dor. pulcherrima x Phal. Zada).

There is considerable variation in the advanced generations, but the reddish color tends to be brilliant, the pastels pleasing, and the whites sparkling. Dtps. Pueblo Jewel (Phal. Dos Pueblos x Dtps. Pink Jewel) can have white flowers with rose colored lips and a natural spread of 3½ inches. Dtps. Jane Sector (Phal. Dos Pueblos x Dtps. Red Coral) can be all white except for yellow marks on the lip.

Certainly the hybrids in the doritis group are jewels that will continue to shine brightly in the future.

Intergeneric crosses to this writing are listed in Chapter X.

Kingiella

Kingiellas are kin to Phalaenopsis, and intrigue growers who prefer miniatures because both plants and flowers are diminutive. Grow them with phalaenopsis.

The plant looks like a little phalaenopsis with foliage generally less than 3 inches long and 2 inches wide. The flowers look like tiny phalaenopsis.

The five species now classified in the genus Kingiella were classified as Doritis until 1917. The name honored Sir George King, Director of the Botanic Gardens, Calcutta and a specialist on Indian orchids.

KINGIELLA PHILIPPINENSIS has six to eight flowers, each one ½ to ¾ inch across, rosy or pale yellow-white with rose pink lines in the lip.

KINGIELLA DECUMBENS has white sepals and petals, the lateral sepals spotted purple at the base, the lip with three purple lobes. It is not common, but is distributed over a wider area (Malaya, India, Ceylon and Java) than any other species in the Phalaenopsis-Doritis-Kingiella complex. Some authorities consider most of the others in the group synonymous with King. decumbens: Phal. hebe, King. philippinensis, King. steffensii, Dor. or Phal. wightii, and Aerides decumbens.

KINGIELLA TAENIALIS has ½ inch mauve-purple flowers. It is deciduous, requires little water in winter and is best grown on a slab.

(Below) Kingiella philippinensis. (Right) Doriella Tiny (Kingiella philippinensis x Doritis pulcherrima).

CHAPTER X

MULTIGENERICS

Phalaenopsis cross with many other genera. A few multigeneric hybrids were made many years ago, but the boom is really on now. This is where the action is, and these are the flowers of the future. They broaden the horizon of the phalaenopsis, adding new colors, forms and plant types to the already vast array of orchids in the world.

A collection of only perfect big white phals is monotonous. And while every collection should have a portion of the perfect whites, there's not a chance of it being dull if it is varied with multigenerics.

Certainly color is a factor. The easy way to yellow in the first generation is by using Renanthera x Phalaenopsis. A new route to white or pink flowers with cherry red lips was by use of Vanda cristata (see Chapter IV). And a route to red is a combination with Renanthera. Take Renanthopsis Yee Peng (Renanthera storiei x Phal. serpentilingua) which has upright spikes of a dozen or more blood-red flowers on an upright semi-terete plant.

Obviously where three or more genera are involved, two of them had been crossed previously to make a bigeneric cross. For instance, Asconopsis is two genera, Phalaenopsis and Ascocentrum. The first cross is Ascps. Mini-Coral (Phal. schilleriana x Asctm. miniatum).

But take Ernestara (Phalaenopsis x Renanthera x Vandopsis.) The first of this genus, Entra. Helga Reuter, is Renanopsis Cape Sable x Phal. Dos Pueblos. Renanopsis is Renanthera x Vandopsis.

To get Ascovandoritis Sonnhild Kitts (Doritis x Ascocentrum x Vanda)

Rhynchonopsis   Melody
(Phalaenopsis Rosy Pam x
Rhynchostylis retusa).

Renanthopsis   Jan   Goo
(Phalaenopsis   sanderiana
x Renanthera monachica).

Renanthopsis Bronze De-
light (Renanthera Brookie
Chandler x Phalaenopsis
Doris).

the parents are Doritis pulcherrima x Ascocenda Red Gem. Ascocenda is Ascocentrum x Vanda.

Similar is Devereuxara (Ascocentrum x Phalaenopsis x Vanda), and the parents of the first hybrid, Dvra. Ellis, are Vandaenopsis Jawaii x Ascocenda Ophelia, making it two parts Vanda, one part Phalaenopsis and one part Ascocentrum. The flower form is like the Ascocenda, the color sometimes dun color like Phalaenopsis serpentilingua. The plant is dainty with nicely curved semi-terete leaves.

If you learn the names and abbreviations, and add to the list as new hybrids are registered, you can follow the development of new genera.

The list, never up to date, invites additions:

Phalaenopsis (Phal.) Multigeneric Hybrids

name of genus	parentage	abbreviation
Aeridopsis (Phalaenopsis x Aerides)		Aerps.
Arachnopsis (Phalaenopsis x Arachnis)		Arnps.
Asconopsis (Phalaenopsis x Ascocentrum)		Ascps.
Beardara (Phalaenopsis x Doritis x Ascocentrum)		Bdra.
Doriellaopsis (Phalaenopsis x Doritis x Kingiella)		Dllps.
Doritaenopsis (Phalaenopsis x Doritis)		Dtps.
Devereuxara (Phalaenopsis x Ascocentrum x Vanda)		Dvra.
Ernestara (Phalaenopsis x Renanthera x Vandopsis)		Entra.
Laycockara (Phalaenopsis x Arachnis x Vandopsis)		Lay.
Moirara (Phalaenopsis x Renanthera x Vanda)		Moir.
Phalaenetia (Phalaenopsis x Neofinetia)		Phnta.
Phalaerianda (Phalaenopsis x Aerides x Vanda)		Phda.
Phalandopsis (Phalaenopsis x Vandopsis)		Phdps.
Renanthopsis (Phalaenopsis x Renanthera)		Rnthps.
Rhynchonopsis (Phalaenopsis x Rhynchostylis)		Rhnps.
Rhyndoropsis (Phalaenopsis x Doritis x Rhynchostylis)		Rhdps.
Sappanara (Phalaenopsis x Arachnis x Renanthera)		Sapp.

PHAL. MULTIGENERICS (Con't.)

name of genus parentage	abbreviation
Sarconopsis (Phalaenopsis x Sarcochilus)	Srnps.
Trevorara (Phalaenopsis x Arachnis x Vanda)	Trev.
Vandaenopsis (Phalaenopsis x Vanda)	Vdnps.
Yapara (Phalaenopsis x Rhynchostylis x Vanda)	Yap.
———— (Phalaenopsis x Doritis x Vanda)	———

Doritis (Dor.) Multigeneric Hybrids

name of genus parentage	abbreviation
Ascovandoritis (Doritis x Ascocentrum x Vanda)	Asvts.
Beardara (Doritis x Phalaenopsis x Ascocentrum)	Bdra.
Doricentrum (Doritis x Ascocentrum)	Dctm.
Doriella (Doritis x Kingiella)	Drlla.
Doriellaopsis (Doritis x Phalaenopsis x Kingiella)	Dllps.
Doritaenopsis (Doritis x Phalaenopsis)	Dtps.
Rhyndoropsis (Doritis x Phalaenopsis x Rhynchostylis)	Rhdps.
Vandoritis (Doritis x Vanda)	Vdts.
———— (Doritis x Aerides)	———
———— (Doritis x Pelantantheria)	———
———— (Doritis x Phalaenopsis x Vanda)	———
———— (Doritis x Rhynchostylis)	———

Kingiella (King.) Multigeneric Hybrids

name of genus parentage	abbreviation
Doriella (Kingiella x Doritis)	Drlla.
Doriellaopsis (Kingiella x Phalaenopsis x Doritis)	Dllps.

CHAPTER XI

POTTING AND REPOTTING

There are many different materials in which phalaenopsis grow well. The choice depends upon what is easily available and not too expensive in your area. Also what your other orchids are potted in.

The point is to use for potting phalaenopsis some material you can get and can manage. All the mixes take different treatment and you have to get the hang of each one.

Osmunda, fir bark, hapuu (tree fern), redwood chips, pumice, aluminum slag, and charcoal are favorites. Some are used in combination, such as bark and redwood fiber, or tree fern and redwood fiber.

In France some growers pot in two parts live sphagnum moss and one part polypodium, plus dried cow manure. In South Africa they use native coarse pine bark and feed every second watering with 30-10-10.

One grower I met in Australia pots his phalaenopsis in the backbone of cuttlefish (squid) which he chops up into half-inch squares and soaks three times to get the salt out.

If you buy plants that are established in some medium new to you and you want to experiment, leave them alone and follow culture directions provided by the person from whom you bought them. If you are happy with the way your other plants are growing, then transfer new plants to the same medium right away so you can treat them the same.

If you find something you think is better than what you are using, try it for at least six months or a year on a few plants before shifting your entire collection.

You must coordinate your environment and your habits with the response of your plants to the potting mixture. If you are heavy handed with the hose, the mixture needs to be very porous. If you

A plant that makes many keikis is attractive grown in a large tree fern basket, the little plants on the stems anchored to the fern with hairpins.

are too busy to water often, it needs to be moisture retentive. If you grow your plants in bright light, you need to water more often than if you grow them in reduced light and the moisture does not evaporate rapidly. Temperature is a factor, too.

Containers

About pots. Some people like clay and some swear by plastic. Here again, the potting mixture, environment and care all enter into the picture. The balance of light, water, temperature and fertilizer is your aim.

Clay pots have an evaporative quality that lessens the danger of overwatering or of persistent wetness that excludes oxygen. Clay pots keep roots cooler by 10° to 15° F. than plastic pots. This is desirable in a location that is hot, as in a home where the room is kept quite warm at night. But it is not desirable where heat is inadequate and plants are likely to be chilled at night.

Plastic pots retain moisture and fertilizer longer, but the danger of retaining too much moisture to the exclusion of air is great. And retention of fertilizer salts, not washed out by thorough watering, can burn roots. But if the air is dry or if the light is bright, plastic may be preferable to clay.

Shallow pots, of whatever material, dry out more rapidly than deeper pots.

**Phalaenopsis Martha. The original plant and two keikis
grow together in a slat basket and make a good show
when they are in bloom.**

Whatever the potting mixture and the container, the roots need
room to run. Phalaenopsis roots are very long on a healthy plant and
run around and around inside the pot or climb over the rim and wrap
around outside. Doritis roots tend to grow straight down as far as
possible rather than around. The pot need not be as wide as the leaf
span of the plant, but neither should it be so small that the plant is
top heavy. Give the roots plenty of room. But on the other hand,
work out a type of potting medium and sufficient crock so that with
your watering schedule the roots will be moist but not soggy. Compost
that is constantly wet is likely to rot the roots and turn sour.

Large plants may be potted in slatted baskets or large treefern
baskets. A slatted basket is good for a grouping, such as a mother
plant and its keikis, or divisions procured by cutting off the top and
persuading the old stump to sprout (see Propagation). The flat tree
fern baskets 12 or 14 inches in diameter are excellent containers for
colonies of Phal. lueddemanniana and others that make many keikis.
Don't sever the keikis from the long stems, merely bend them around
to fit into the basket and anchor them with hairpins. A full basket
of Phal. lueddemanniana var. pulchra plants in bloom is gorgeous.

Other containers are bonsai pots, decorative pots if they have drainage, and various hanging containers.

Or you can take a tree fern log, say 4 inches in diameter and 15
inches long and secure several plants to it. Hang it vertically or

horizontally. It accommodates half a dozen small plants, a bouquet when in bloom. My plants of Golden Louis and others of the early yellows now grow on logs, leaving bench space for individual pots of newer crosses.

You can make a sensational grouping of phalaenopsis in a strawberry jar. If it is a very large jar, use many large crocks and a very porous potting mixture to facilitate drainage, and be sure to knock drainage holes in the bottom. It is most effective if the plants are all alike.

Remember that in nature phalaenopsis are gregarious, sharing a tree limb with other phalaenopsis, orchids and epiphytes.

Hanging containers dry out faster than crowded pots and need watering more often.

WHEN TO REPOT — Frequency of repotting depends upon the durability of the potting medium. When it starts to break down so that it holds water too long, or when the plant needs more space, it is time to repot. Otherwise, do not disturb. Some of the large barks last a few years, other materials may get soft within a year. Some of the inert materials never change character.

Seedlings in small pots need at least yearly repotting to larger containers if they are well grown. Plant groups in large baskets may never need to be moved, only to have the old material shaken out and replaced. Plants on logs need no attention until the log disintegrates.

You can repot phalaenopsis at any time that the plants seem to be in active growth. This is most evident in summer, but since they have no pseudobulbs, phalaenopsis keep right on growing almost all the time. When you see new roots emerging it is a sign of activity, and a good time to repot so the new roots go into the new medium.

HOW TO REPOT — Shake the plant out of the pot. If necessary, run a knife around inside the rim to loosen the roots.

Remove all of the old potting medium. Cut off any dead, dry roots but leave all good roots alone. Choose a container big enough to fit them into. Cut off the old stump below the good roots.

Have ready a pot of suitable size and clean crock. Hold the plant in position at the level you want it to grow with the lower leaves just above the rim of the pot. Fill around with the potting material, working it with your fingers or a blunt instrument around the roots. If necessary, use a pot clip to hold the plant down until the roots take hold.

Do not water until the next day to give broken roots a chance to heal.

CHAPTER XII

PROPAGATION

Phalaenopsis are monopodial and therefore do not offer the opportunities for making two plants from one that the sympodial plants do. However, it is possible to get additional plants by a few methods.

Division

When a phalaenopsis grows up so that there is a visible length of stem between the potting mixture and the leaves, with new roots near the leaves, you can divide it into two plants.

Cut off the top portion by slicing horizontally through the woody stem below the leaves and the new roots but above where some old roots leave the stem.

Pot the top up separately. Leave the headless stump alone in its old pot. Set it in the shade in a humid place and do not water it.

In several weeks, maybe longer, one or two little plants will emerge from the sides of the old stump. Remember there are dormant buds along the stem that can become flowers or plants, and by removing the top, some should activate into new vegetative growths.

When the little plants have roots of their own long enough to reach into the potting mixture, slice the plants from the stem where they are attached and pot them up separately. Treat them like seedlings.

When a phalaenopsis plant becomes leggy, cut off the top (including a few upper roots) and pot this up as a new plant. Do not disturb the stump and it may sprout.

Growth stages of doritis plants in flask and community pots.

Or pot them along with the previous top into a large container or basket to make a group of identical plants. Let the old stump sit where it is. It might make more new offsets.

Occasionally a plant will make a keiki or plantlet from its stem, maybe even between its leaves. Either break it loose when it has roots or leave it where it is.

Occasionally a keiki on a large-flowered phalaenopsis appears on the flower spike. Cut the stem below it when the keiki has roots and pot it up separately.

The many keikis on the Phal. lueddemanniana types can be trained to grow in the same container with the original mother plant or can be cut off when they have roots.

Stem Propagation

Another method of making vegetative or identical propagations of phalaenopsis is by encouraging a node on a flower stem to grow into a plant. This is often done with awarded cultivars, and the new plant carries the award also.

The procedure includes sterilized equipment and a seed-sowing box like used for planting flasks. Don't try to make stem propagations without the precautions and the equipment as some of them become contaminated even with the best of preparation.

Stem propagation two months old in bottle; another six months old in a pot two weeks after removed from bottle.

Cut the basal piece of the flower stem containing a good eye so there is ½ inch of stem above the node and 1¼ inch below. Remove the bract around the bud. Sterilize the stem and, working in the flasking case, inset it into a bottle of agar as for seeds with the node slightly above the agar. Stopper and label the bottle, using a separate bottle for each stem.

The stem should make a plant with leaves and roots within six months. Transfer it from the bottle to a pot and treat like a seedling.

Meristem Culture

Propagation of phalaenopsis plants by meristem tissue culture has not been as successful percentagewise as some other genera. However, the process will be more nearly perfected as time goes on.

Since removing the growing point of a monopodial plant would destroy it, the tissue used for meristemming phalaenopsis comes from inside the dormant buds along the bottom of the flower stems, the same as for stem propagations, and from the dormant buds along the main stem between the leaves.

Phalaenopsis From Seeds

You can self or cross your phalaenopsis by taking the pollen from the front of the column and inserting it back into the stigmatic cavity.

First consider if the plant you self-pollinate is of good enough quality to warrant reproducing. Or if the two phalaenopsis or related orchids that you want to cross pollinate might produce flowers with desirable characteristics.

To gather the pollen use a small pointed stick such as a wooden match sharpened to a point. Hook it under the anther cap at the front of the column and pull. You will dislodge the cap and the yellow pollinia behind it. (See sketches.)

Discard the cap. The pollinia have a sticky substance which will probably hold them to the match, but take the precaution of working

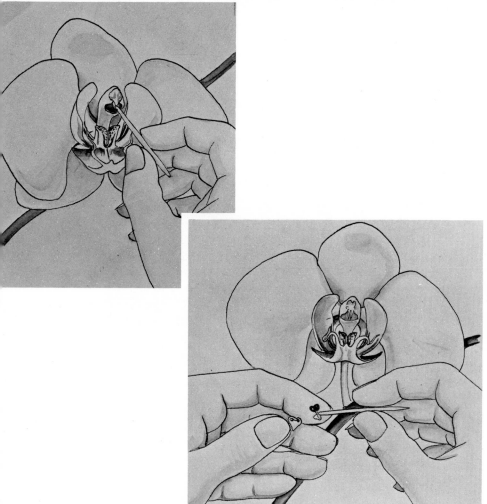

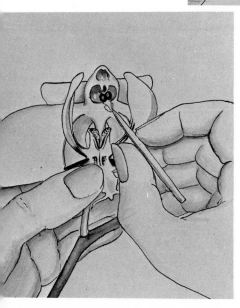

To pollinate a phalaenopsis-type flower:

1. Remove anther cap.
2. Separate the pollen.
3. Insert pollen in stigma.

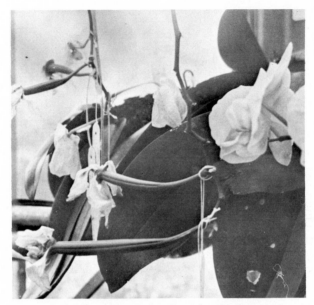

Seed pods form behind withered flowers.

on a table or other solid surface in case you drop the pollinia. If you drop pollen in a greenhouse all is lost.

Insert one mass of pollen (pollinia) into the stigma. This is the cavity in the underside of the column behind the rostellum. The rostellum is a barrier that separates the anther from the stigma. The cavity is sticky and with a few tries the pollen should stick to it and pull loose from the match.

Within a few days the flower will wither and the ovary in the pedicel between the flower and the main flower stalk will begin to swell. It may develop into a fat seed pod, or it may change color and fall off.

Green pod or ovule culture or embryo culture is the method of sowing the seed before the pod comes to complete maturity and cracks open. The seed are more viable, but timing is important.

Most flowers other than orchids have a fully developed ovary and an egg or eggs ready for fertilization when the flower opens. Not so with orchids. When the flower opens the ovary is only partially developed, and actual fertilization does not take place for 55 to 70 days in Doritis pulcherrima and 65 to 80 days in Phalaenopsis Chieftan.

The earliest growth of cultures is reported from five to 10 days later, but it is best to add 10 to 15 days to these figures before harvesting the pods.*

The process of sowing the seed is detailed in YOU CAN GROW CATTLEYA ORCHIDS and not repeated here. You can work with a plastic bag, as described there, or make yourself an inexpensive flasking box from a cardboard carton. Choose a box three feet square. Cut the sides on a slant so it is 3 feet high at the back and 12 inches high at the front. Line the inside with aluminum foil and cover the top tightly with transparent plastic film. Cut two round holes in the 1-foot front for your hands. Secure plastic bags, open at both ends, to the openings.

Sterilize the inside of the box, your equipment and your hands. Put your hands through the holes and fasten the plastic sleeves around your wrists with rubber bands.

If you don't want to go to the trouble of flasking your own seed there are laboratories that will do it for you.

Keep the flasks in subdued light and warm temperature. Reflask as the little plants grow, putting fewer plants into more bottles to give them room.

Then transfer the small plants to community pots, also located in less light than mature plants. As the pots become crowded, transfer plants to larger communities or to individual pots.

---

* From Embryo Culture of Orchids by Yoneo Sagawa and Helen L. Calmayor in the Proceedings of the Fifth World Orchid Conference.

**Phalaenopsis are spectacular growing in a large strawberry jar.
Home of Mr. and Mrs. J. Y. Arnold, Palm Beach, Florida.**

CHAPTER XIII

PROBLEMS

Phalaenopsis have relatively few problems and most of those are easily controlled.

You will never have all of the problems and pests described and illustrated here. Some are more prevalent in certain countries. Some that are not yet present in your country may be stopped at the border with fumigation of imported plants. Never sneak orchids in. You might infest your collection and your country with some new problem.

Identity

Plant problems are of three types: pests, diseases and physiological disturbances. Identify any problem before you attempt to control it. No use in treating a disease with an insecticide. You waste time and money.

Study the drawings and descriptions of pests in this chapter and you will be able to identify most of the intruders on all the orchids in your collection. Some pests are big enough to see, others may be visible beneath a magnifying glass. Others are recognized by their damage.

Some of the diseases can be identified by the photographs. The only way to absolutely identify virus is by a laboratory test which your governmental officials or university may do. Not all leaf problems or flower color irregularities are virus diseases. Do not throw out a plant unless you are sure. The leaf problem may be caused by tiny mites, and the color break in the blossoms due to genetic or pest disturbance.

The physiological problems may be due to poor culture. Admit that if you have not watered enough the lower leaves may shrivel and fall off, the flower buds dry up or the roots die. Other problems result from overwatering or humidity that is too high. If you consider the possibility that you may be at fault, you may be able to correct the problem.

Environmental problems of air pollution, too many cloudy days, or colder or hotter weather than you can offset may be beyond control but should be recognized for what they are.

Pest Controls

The chemicals are changing so rapidly that we are not giving recommendations by trade or chemical names. The laws regulating chemicals change constantly, further confusing the issue.

Once you have identified your pest from the drawings and descriptions in this book, get a pesticide that says on its label that it specifically eliminates that pest. Buy from orchid catalogs or local nurseries or garden shops. If in doubt, consult a government entomologist for a recommendation.

These are the categories of pest control chemicals:

CONTACT INSECTICIDE kills on contact. It must touch the pest. In a colony of thousands of scales you must sufficiently coat the area with spray or dust to reach each one. Contact insecticides are used on pests that suck or chew.

STOMACH POISON kills the pest when he eats it. It is useful for critters that chew but not for those that suck.

SYSTEMIC INSECTICIDE penetrates the plant tissues and controls pests that suck or chew. A systemic travels all through the plant and may be applied as a drench to the roots, a spray to the foliage, or a dip for the entire plant. If you drench, flood the pot. If you dip, hold the plant under until it bubbles. Wear rubber gloves so you don't get the chemical on your hands. Some systemics seem to penetrate the human body and may cause dizziness or other ill effects.

MITICIDE is necessary to control mites because they are not insects. Some systemics, if so labeled, include miticide.

Some preparations are combinations of insecticide-miticide-fungicide. Most of those for roses are good for orchids.

Our vocabulary of problem controls contains many words ending in "-cide." This combination of letters is borrowed from the Latin "cida" meaning "cutter, killer" from "caldere" which translates "to cut" or "to kill." So pesticide kills pests; insecticide kills insects; molluscacide controls mollusks such as snails; fungicide for fungus; miticide for mites.

Disease controls are discussed with the problems.

APPLICATION OF CHEMICALS: It is easy to apply the chemicals for pest and disease control. Ready-mixed aerosols or squeeze containers are useful in small collections. Some chemicals are easy to mix with water.

There are many types of applicators: attachments to fasten to the garden hose, spray top bottles, hand operated sprayers with which you build up air pressure with a handle like pumping up a bicycle tire, and large pressure sprayers for big operations.

Be sure to clean the equipment thoroughly after each use. Never spray plants with a sprayer previously used for weedkiller for the lawn.

Mixing pesticides is of utmost importance. Too little does no good and too much may do great harm. This is especially true of systemics, which are absorbed by the plant and cannot be washed off. There's a lot we don't know about the newer chemicals, systemic and pseudo-systemic. Some growers have had crippled phalaenopsis flowers and distorted flower spikes after using systemics or antibiotics. It is possible that they used too much too often, that the plants were too dry or too wet when it was applied, or that the timing was bad with relation to the initiation or development of the inflorescence. We don't know. If you are trying any new material, use it on a few plants and watch them closely for several weeks for unusual developments.

Small smoke bombs for fumigating small greenhouses are easy to use.

Follow the directions exactly that are on the container of any brand you buy as the formulas vary. Take heed of precautions about applying chemicals at low or high temperatures. Repeat applications as often, but no oftener, than indicated.

Take all precautions for your own safety as many of the chemicals are toxic to people. Even the safest is a killer, and might do you harm. Wear rubber or plastic gloves, long sleeves, long pants and a rain hat, even a plastic raincoat and a mask if so directed. Do not smoke or eat while spraying until you thoroughly wash your hands and face. Remove and wash all your clothes down to the skin after using a large power spray. Wearing gloves and eyeglasses should suffice if you are using hand operated equipment.

Prevention of Problems

Keep your plant area clean so pests can't hide. Sterilize your pots and tools so you don't transmit diseases.

Use individual razor knives for cutting flower stems and either throw them away or sterilize them. You can pick single blooms by hand.

Pick off dead foliage and throw it out. Cut off flowers as they fade. Don't go through the greenhouse fingering first one plant and then another. You might transmit a disease to a healthy plant with your hands.

Be vigilant. Pick up and inspect every plant as often as possible. Look under the leaves. Inspect each new plant before you buy it, and take a hard look at gift plants before accepting them. Don't introduce problems.

Wash green algae from greenhouse glass and off the pots.

Grow your plants as well as possible. Healthy plants, like healthy people, can resist some of the problems.

Problems of the Foliage

THE PESTS

SCALE INSECTS are not as prevalent on phalaenopsis as on cattleyas, where Boisduval scale can cover a pseudobulb like icing on a cake.

Scales are sucking insects. They have piercing mouthparts that penetrate the plant tissue and siphon out the juices.

Scales on the upper surface of a leaf are clearly visible, but they may remain undetected on the underside until the leaf turns silvery or yellowish on top.

Soft scales, armored scales and mealybugs, are problems of phalaenopsis. Those classed as soft scales may have coats as hard as armored scales. On the armored scales the hard cover is not part of the body, with soft scales it is. The chitinous cover, which gives them the name of tortoise scales, may be translucent or opaque, dull or glossy.

The females do the damage. They lay eggs or give birth to living young beneath the shields. The crawlers move about for a few days then settle in one place for the rest of their lives.

Soft scales secrete honeydew on which sooty mold grows so smutty foliage is a clue. (See Fungus Diseases.)

Brown soft scale (Coccus hesperidum) is a world-wide problem on ornamentals, orchids and fruits in greenhouses and warm climates. It infests gardenias, ferns, apples, poinsettias, roses, ivy, palms, etc.

The female is flat and oval, about ⅛ inch long, green or brown camouflaged by the leaf color. Appearing flat on top, the shield is concave underneath to protect the young. It may be marbled or ridged. Look for pinhead-size pimples on the leaf surfaces, singly or in colonies.

The mother gives birth to one or two live young every day for a month. They mature in two months.

Hemispherical scale (Saissetia coffeae or S. hemisphaerica) is easy to identify because the female is a glossy brown hump and looks like a tiny turtle with a ruffle around it. It is about ⅛ inch in diameter, but you need a magnifying glass to see the ruffle.

This soft scale is a problem on many ornamentals, particularly ferns and palms. Each female lays several hundred eggs which hatch at different times requiring repetition of the control.

Proteus scale (Parlatoria proteus) is an armored scale of world-wide distribution on tropical plants.

The adult female's armor is 1/25 to 1/12 inch in length, an elongated oval, slightly convex. It is brownish or greenish yellow with lighter margins. Partial to strap-leaf orchids, it is found on phalaenopsis.

Orchid soft scale or false brown scale (Coccus pseudohesperidum) infests only orchids, especially cattleyas and dendrobiums in some countries. It does not develop such large populations as the brown soft scale.

Control of scales: Contact insecticide kills the scales when directly applied, systemic insecticide gets them through the plant juices. Repeat applications of either type of chemical in order to reach the crawlers as they depart from the mother since the contact may not kill them under the shield and the systemic will not reach them until they begin to suck juice. Follow timing directions on the brand you use.

MEALYBUGS are soft scales. Their pink or yellow bodies are covered with powdery secretions that make them look like white felt. They generally have white filaments like fringe.

Adult female mealybugs are generally oval, 1/15 to 1/5 inch in length. Some species lay eggs in cottony sacs and some give birth to living young.

Each female lays 100 to 600 eggs during one or two weeks. Eggs may hatch in 10 days to 10 weeks. The crawlers are oval, light yellow with six-legged smooth bodies. When they begin to feed, the waxy filaments start forming and radiate in 36 projections like legs. Mealybugs are sluggish but can move.

In time the males change into winged insects like flies and do not feed.

Mealybugs suck sap and produce honeydew.

The long-tailed mealybug (Pseudococcus adonidum) is partial to phalaenopsis plants. It is readily distinguishable by two threads at the posterior end that are as long as the body. It is a problem on avocado, citrus and many other tropical, house plants and greenhouse plants. It produces living young.

The orchid mealybug (Pseudococcus microcirculus) has tail filaments slightly longer than those around the body but not as long as the long-tailed mealybug. It lays 100-200 yellowish eggs in a cottony white sac. The eggs hatch in two weeks. The crawlers are mature in six to eight weeks.

Control of mealybugs: Mealybugs have many natural enemies including lacewings.

Since mealybugs can be seen with the naked eye, in a small collection you can touch them individually with a cotton swab dipped in alcohol (nail polish remover or lighter fluid.)

Contact insecticide, thoroughly applied, should control the type that has living young, and a systemic insecticide may be residual long enough to kill the crawlers when they begin to eat.

Keep a close check on plants you grow with orchids, such as African violets, crotons, and fuchsias, which are infested by these pests. Some species of mealybugs are hardy outdoors in New York, so check garden plants. Control ants, which move mealybugs around.

APHIDS. The world is so full of aphids that it is almost impossible to distinguish one species from another. For instance, there are more than 100 different kinds of aphids in the western part of the United States, and the melon or cotton aphid in the southeast feeds on a hundred different host plants.

An aphid is a sucking insect with a soft pear-shaped body, less than ⅛ inch in length. It has antennae, six legs, and a pair of cornicles like horns on its rear end. It has a hollow beak enclosing four needle-like stylets which it inserts into plant tissue for sucking sap.

There are winged and wingless forms of aphids. There are viviparous types which bear living young and oviparous aphids which lay eggs. Sometimes one type aphid will produce living nymphs in warm weather and lay eggs for overwintering. The viviparous females reproduce without fertilization by a male. In warm climates, homes or greenhouses living young may be produced all year. A female may give birth to 100 offspring which are adults within a week, mostly females. Hot dry conditions favor aphid multiplication.

When a plant becomes overpopulated, the winged aphids depart to colonize on other plants.

Aphids are called plant lice, greenflies, blackflies and other localized names. They actually come in many colors. One called the orchid aphid (Cerataphis orchideaum) has nymphs that are dark and round like disks with white fringe around their bodies.

Aphids cause plants to become sickly and the leaves to curl or pucker. They are partial to new growth or seedlings. Their honeydew smuts the foliage and is a substratum for sooty mold fungus.

Control of aphids: Nicotine sulfate has been a reliable aphid control for many years. Newer contact and systemic insecticides are equally effective. Repeat as directed. Be vigilant as winged aphids may continually reinfest the plants. Parasites and predators help control aphids. See Friends.

THRIPS infest flowers and foliage.

Discolored or disfigured foliage, especially new leaves and tender seedlings, may indicate that thrips are present.

They are so slender that you are more likely to see tiny specks of excrement before you spot the thrips. Hold suspected foliage up to a strong light and you may see damaged translucent areas. They may become rusty or black.

Thrips devitalize plants by rasping the cells and sucking up the juices that seep out.

Note that the word thrips is both singular and plural. Thrips are seldom seen singly.

These are possible pests of phalaenopsis foliage.

Greenhouse thrips (Heliothrips haemorrhoidalis) are world wide on tropical plants. They attack only foliage and fruits, causing leaves to look bleached, silvery or papery, and sometimes to fall off. They insert their eggs just beneath the epidermis causing blisters.

These thrips are blackish brown with yellow legs, 1/24 inch long. They have networks of lines over their heads and bodies. The dots of excrement are reddish black.

The banded greenhouse thrips (Hercinothrips femoralis) and the red-banded thrips (Selenothrips rubrocinctus) from the West Indies are similar to greenhouse thrips. The first is dark brown or black with reddish yellow head and fore part of the body, and dusty white wings. The latter is brown or black with a bright red band across the body.

Control of thrips: Any contact or systemic insecticide used for scales should control thrips simultaneously.

BEETLES (Weevils) have heads prolonged downward into long snouts which have mouth parts at the ends. Hawaii and Malaya have beetles that attack phalaenopsis plants. These are small black snout weevils (all weevils are beetles) 1/12 to 1/2 inch long. They can fly, having a pair of membraneous wings beneath their shiny hard covering wings.

Snout beetles drill holes into the young growing tips of several types of orchids and lay eggs in the holes. The eggs hatch into larvae that feed on plant tissues causing internal damage and chlorotic or blackened areas. They also attack roots and flowers.

Not all beetles are plant pests. There are about a quarter of a million species of beetles. Some eat other insects. (See Friends.)

In the Philippines the orchid beetle (Crioceris semipunctata) is a pest of phalaenopsis leaves and flowers. It is snoutless, yellow and about ½ inch long.

Control of beetles: Systemics do not seem to eliminate the beetles nor reach the grubs, but contact insecticides can be used as the adults are seen and identified as enemies.

PLANT BUGS are plentiful but only one is recorded as a specific pest of phalaenopsis, Mertila malayensis.

Known in the East Indies, Burma and the Philippines, the orchid bug that attacks phalaenopsis is 1/5 inch long when mature, has a red head, yellow wings and a black body.

Adults and young bugs puncture leaves and suck juices, causing pale spots on the foliage. A generation matures in about 43 days.

Other orchid bugs of the genus Tenthecoris, found in the U.S., Europe, Central and South America on other orchids are red or orange with blue wings, about 1/6 inch long.

Control of plant bugs: contact insecticide.

MITES are particularly destructive to phalaenopsis. The succulent foliage attracts them, and the horizontal leaves offer hiding places on the undersides unless you regularly turn them over for inspection. Even so, the mites are so tiny they are extremely difficult to see.

Mites have soft bodies, some less than 1/50 or 1/100 inch long. They may be red, yellowish or greenish. Some spin webs over the surface of the foliage, not suspended in space like normal spider webs, which may be visible. Mites shed their skins as they molt, and these tiny dark bits of debris may be visible if present in large numbers on leaf surfaces.

Generally, the clue to mites is the damage. The leaves begin to show yellow flecks, the spots become sunken and run together to form large pitted areas that are minus their green color appearing dirty grey or brownish. Leaves twist and shrivel and fall off. Since mites on other orchids cause leaves to discolor but not to fall as rapidly as they do

Pests of foliage and roots which infest many types of orchids.

A. Proteus scale

B. Brown soft scale

C. Orchid soft scale

D. Hemispherical scale

E. Mealybug

F. Long-tailed mealybug

G. Red spider mite

H. False spider mite

I. Thrips

J. Ants

K. Termites

L. Sowbug- pillbug

M. Springtails

N. Aphids

O. Plant bug

P. Snout beetle

Q. Bush snails

R. Philippine orchid beetle

S. Fuzzy caterpillar

T. Smooth caterpillar

U. Grasshopper

V. Slug

W. Snail

X. Worm

Y. Millipede

Z. Cockroaches

AA. Centipede

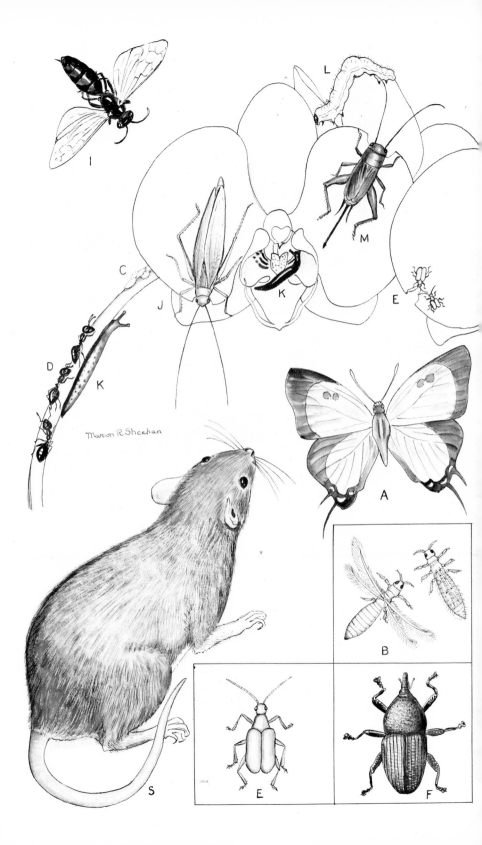

Marion R. Sheehan

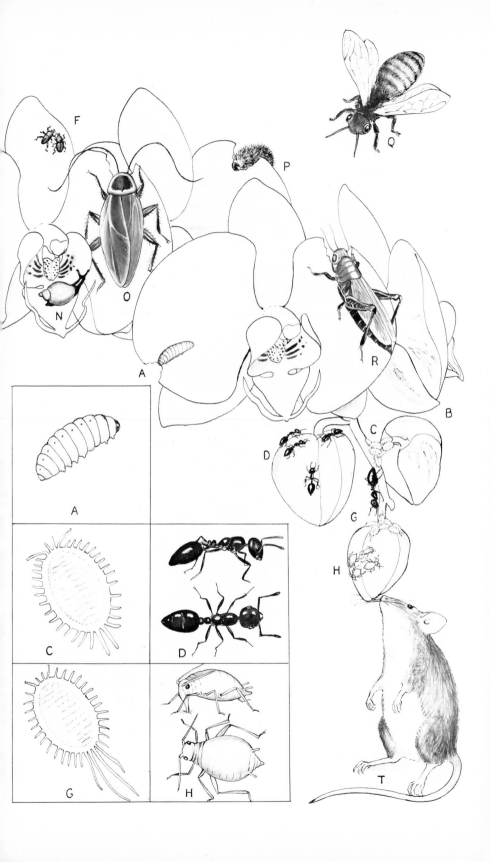

Pests of the flowers (opposite). Identify them and then eliminate them.

A. Hairstreak butterfly and larvae

B. Thrips

C. Mealybug

D. Ants

E. Philippine orchid beetle

F. Snout beetle

G. Long-tailed mealybug

H. Aphids

I. Wasp

J. Katydid

K. Slugs

L. Cabbage looper

M. Cricket

N. Snail

O. Cockroach

P. Fuzzy caterpillar

Q. Bee

R. Grasshopper

S. Rat

T. Mouse

on phalaenopsis, it is possible the mites poison the phalaenopsis foliage.

The two-spotted mite (Tetranychus urticae) is the most common of the mites we call red spider. It is not necessarily red. It is a garden and greenhouse pest on many plants, especially cymbidiums. It spins webs.

The female lays 100 to 200 eggs on the undersides of the foliage during a period of three to four weeks. At high temperatures these become adults in five days. In greenhouses there is a new generation year round, every three or four weeks. Mites thrive in high humidity and stagnant air. Crowded plants reduce air circulation around themselves and encourage mites.

The phalaenopsis mite (Tenuipalpus pacificus) is called a false spider mite because it does not spin webs. It is a serious pest of ferns and orchids around the world. It was found first on phalaenopsis, hence the name. It is a problem in Australia, Java, Thailand, the Philippines, the United States and in Central and South America where it originated. False spider mites were noted in England in 1859 on orchids and are still there.

This mite is red, about 1/100th of an inch long and thus invisible to the eye. The female lays red eggs at the rate of one or two a day. They hatch in a week and are adults in two more weeks.

Control of mites: The first step in control is to identify the problem. Many growers get excited when the foliage starts changing color and immediately assume the plant has virus. I have had any number of leaves tested for virus only to have the problem identified as mites. Since mites are hard to see, unless you can spot the webs or the cast skins with a hand magnifying glass, you may be able to discover them by rubbing a white tissue or handkerchief over the leaf surface, both underside and above, as the false spider mites accumulate on both sides. If the cloth shows reddish streaks, mites are present.

Being animals and not insects, insecticides seldom eliminate mites. Use a specific miticide or acaricide. Since not all miticides kill the eggs apply at least two sprayings 7 to 10 days apart to reach the young mites as they hatch. Some of the systemics control mites if repeated as directed, because the mites have resting stages when they don't eat.

Syringing foliage, especially undersides, with the hose knocks off some mites if the force is strong enough to break the webs but not strong enough to damage the foliage.

Do not be hasty about throwing out a plant that has lost all its leaves, possibly from mite damage. Apply a miticide to the crown. Then set the damaged or leafless plant in a warm, shady place. Very likely new, healthy leaves will appear from the crown and develop normally if you continue to control the mites.

SNAILS AND SLUGS make slimy trails across foliage and chew wavy grooves into the leaf surfaces or ragged holes on through. For more details, see Flower Pests.

The giant African snail invades other countries and has a fondness for fleshy foliage. A plant may be defoliated in a night and the snail hiding somewhere cool and moist the next day. This snail has a shell up to 8 inches long and the body extending another 4 inches, and it may live nine years.

GRASSHOPPERS AND CATERPILLARS chew foliage in unsightly patterns. Pick them off by hand. If you are squeamish, use a clothespin.

THE DISEASES

Foliage diseases may not be limited to foliage, where the symptoms show up, but may affect roots too.

If possible, distinguish the nature of a disease—whether caused by bacteria, fungus or virus—in order to treat it with a suitable chemical or have it tested for virus.

BACTERIAL DISEASES occur when bacteria enter leaves through their stomata or through wounds made by insects or by people.

Brown spot, leaf spot or brown rot (Pseudomonas cattleyae) is a more serious disease of phalaenopsis than it is of cattleyas. The diseased areas exude infectious material which may spread rapidly to other plants in splashing water. Seedlings and community pots are particularly susceptible.

The first symptoms are soft water-soaked spots on the foliage, later turning brown or black. If the disease spreads to the growing point it is generally fatal.

Soft rot (Erwinea carotovora) is a common disease of garden plants and vegetables in storage. It enters through wounds, spreads rapidly in warm wet weather or closed environments. It is especially destructive to cattleyas but sometimes spreads to phalaenopsis and other orchids.

The first signs are water soaked spots darker green than normal, and wilting of the leaf. If the leaf breaks off or you touch the surface and break the epidermis, the contaminated juice may run out on the bench or neighboring plants.

Control of bacterial diseases: Some preparations are three-way bactericide-fungicide-algicides. Antibiotics are bactericides which also help control certain fungi. Products sold for control of damping-off diseases of seedlings may be useful for control of problems on mature plants.

Where bacterial or fungal diseases are a problem, use a bactericide or fungicide as a protectant, spraying the collection at directed intervals.

When infection appears, cut back behind it as soon as it is noticed and destroy the amputated portion of the leaf. Sterilize your knife between each plant, or use disposable razor blade knives. Disinfect the bench with a bactericide.

FUNGUS DISEASES are caused by fungi which are organisms without chlorophyll which reproduce by spores.

European anthracnose (Gloeosporium affine) shows up as distinct dead areas on the leaf, circular, slightly sunken, and yellowish or lighter green than normal. The spots turn light brown and under humid conditions reddish masses of slime spores ooze out. These can be spread by wind and water or by handling wet plants to other plants which they enter through a mechanical or insect wound.

Plants that are soft from too much nitrogenous fertilizer are susceptible to this disease, but crisp well-grown plants are reasonably resistant.

Crown rot or Southern blight (Pellicularia rolfsii) is world-wide on many plants in warm areas but only a minor problem on orchids. Cycnoches, phaius and cymbidiums also get it.

This rot first appears on roots and lower leaves. First there is a creamy-yellow discolored area which turns brown and can be diagnosed by the small brown sclerotia the size and color of mustard seeds.

Sooty mold (Capnodium citri) is a fungus that looks like soot on the leaves. It is prevalent on orchids outdoors near citrus or other plants that are hosts of scales and whiteflies that secrete honeydew in which the fungus grows.

If orchid leaves are smutty, first control the pests that encourage it, then wipe off the mold. This fungus does not enter plant tissues, but coats the surface and prevents light from reaching the leaves, which interferes with the process of photosynthesis.

See also section on fungus diseases of the roots which cause foliage to look sick.

Control of fungus diseases: Destroy badly infected plants. To save a valuable plant, remove all potting medium and sterilize the pot. Steam sterilize fresh potting mixture to eliminate any sclerotia that cling to the roots.

Dip or spray infected plants with a bacterio-fungicide or antibiotic. Spray healthy plants to inhibit the development of fungus spores. Coverage is important. Add a drop or two of liquid detergent to the spray to break the surface tension.

Dust or spray the cut surface of any amputated leaf areas with fungicide. Generally fungicide recommended for roses is good for orchids.

Systemic fungicides reach fungi inside the thick leaves of orchids that surface fungicides cannot penetrate. They are useful in killing fungi that cause leaf-spotting diseases including Cercospora on phalaenopsis hybrids. The number of applications at exact intervals is important. (For details see article by Harry Burnett, AOS Bulletin, Vol. 40, April 1971.)

A word of caution. Some phalaenopsis have crippled spikes and flowers after use of some systemics. This may be due to the fact that some chemicals, especially Benomyl, are toxic to the beneficial Rhizoctiona fungus in the potting mixtures on which the orchid plants may be somewhat dependent. So unless labels recommend dipping or drenching of orchids, apply only to foliage in such a fine mist that very little drips onto the potting mix.

Standing water in the top of a phalaenopsis plant leads to fungus problems, particularly crown rot, in seasons or climates when the temperature is low at night. Water overhead with a fine mist only. Hang plants at a slant so water runs out of the crowns.

VIRUS DISEASES are the subject of much discussion.

European anthracnose fungus (Gloeosperum affine).

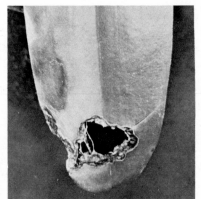

Bacterial brown rot (Pseudomonas cattleyae)

Physiological problem due to some type of burn.

Plant on left has virus,
plant on right does not.

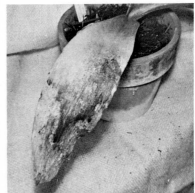

Cymbidium mosaic virus.

Distorted color but not
due to virus.

Cymbidium mosaic virus, common on many genera, does not affect flowers of phalaenopsis except that infected plants are weak and bloom poorly. This disease causes new phalaenopsis leaves to turn yellow in oval or elongated streaks and the yellow spaces on the lower surfaces to become sunken and turn purple-black as the leaves reach mature size. Leaves fall off if the infection is severe.

Tobacco mosaic virus "O" strain (for orchid) attacks many orchids including phalaenopsis but it may not show any symptoms that can be distinguished. Plants are unhealthy if the disease is advanced, but it may be present in a mild form without causing alarm.

Control of virus diseases: Don't panic at every leaf spot. If you suspect virus, have plant tissue analyzed, and throw it out if the test is positive. Otherwise, give it the benefit of the doubt.

There is no cure for virus disease. All you can do is try to avoid it. Buy only healthy looking plants from reputable sources. Take care not to damage plants in handling.

Since phalaenopsis are rarely divided, the danger of spreading virus in routine operations is in cutting the flower spike of a diseased plant and then cutting the spike of a healthy plant. If sap from the virus is on the knife and touches the open stem of the next plant, the infection is spread. Either disinfect the knife between every cut or use an individual razor-blade knife for each plant, then discard or disinfect it.

MISCELLANEOUS PROBLEMS OF THE FOLIAGE

Discoloration of foliage or wilting or limpness of leaves that cannot be traced to pests or diseases may be due to poor culture. Too much or not enough water, poor drainage, watering when temperature is low with cold water, any of these may make plants look unhappy.

Sunburn causes damage to foliage where the rays hit. Calcium deficiency is sometimes mistaken for sunburn.

Chemical injury due to improper mixing or application of fertilizers, pesticides, or disease controls can't be cured. Read the labels all the way through.

Lack of light, dry air, low temperature, high temperature combined with dry air (common indoors) are all environmental factors that make plants look sick.

Problems of the Flowers

THE PESTS

Some of the flower pests are also foliage pests and have been described. They may infest blooms or flower spikes, even under bracts over dormant buds on the spikes.

Check the label of any chemical before applying it to buds or open blooms or the control may do more damage than the pest. Sometimes weaker dilutions are recommended for use on flowers. If in doubt, test the product on a few blooms and watch them for a few days.

MEALYBUGS may gather where the pedicel (stalk of the individual flower) joins the flower spike.

APHIDS sometimes congregate on the flower buds and look like little bumps. Wipe them off gently with soft tissue or cotton. Aphids cause flowers to be crippled, discolored, or to fail to open.

THRIPS are so tiny they are hard to see but their damage to flowers resembles color break virus. No need to destroy a plant unless the virus tests positive, as another year the blooms may be perfect.

Thrips-infested buds fail to open or flowers are deformed. Flowers have brown streaks where thrips are feeding, or are unevenly discolored in other patterns.

Each female thrips lays up to 50 eggs in tender tissue of flowers, buds or stems. These eggs hatch in one to three weeks. The larvae feed, then molt, and in cold climates hibernate on the soil surface outdoors. In some species the life cycle is completed in two weeks with several generations a year.

The flower thrips (Frankliniella) are known to gardeners who grow roses, irises, peonies and daylilies but their activities are not confined to these hosts. Thrips can fly and are transported by wind, infest garden and weed flowers, and get into your house or greenhouse through the screens.

Control of flower thrips: A systemic insecticide reaches thrips inside flower buds. Contact insecticide controls those on the outside of buds or on open flowers if you spray or dust back and front of blooms. Thrips in the area return to the orchids as fast as you get rid of them.

SLUGS AND SNAILS are mollusks, kin to oysters and clams. Each one has a soft unsegmented body, two pairs of tentacles for seeing and smelling. Its mouth is equipped with a rasping file-like tongue called a radula. It has a mucous gland under the body that spreads a slimy trail on which the critter slides its muscular foot and provides a sure clue.

Snails have hard shells of varying shapes and sizes into which they can retreat for protection. Slugs are snails without shells, generally dark in color, some of them spotted, ranging in size from ¼ inch to 7 or 8 inches, but generally about 2 inches long.

Both snails and slugs are night feeders, hiding by day in dark, moist places. They may be active on cloudy days. They require moisture to survive and hence are attracted to phalaenopsis and other orchids where the potting medium is kept moist.

These mollusks are hermaphroditic, each slug and snail having reproductive organs of both sexes, so with reciprocal mating and self-fertilization their reproductive possibilities are enormous. Each slug can lay several hundred tiny jelly-like eggs in groups of about 50 at a time in moist soil. Eggs hatch in a few weeks, but what helps to keep the population down is that some slugs and snails need a year to mature.

Control of snails and slugs: There are molluscacides available. Bear in mind that these pests are not insects and insecticides are generally inadequate. The standard for years has been metaldehyde bait placed around the plants at night. Do not apply metaldehyde dusts or sprays to orchid flowers.

The most effective slug bait is fresh or stale beer! Experiments by the U.S. Department of Agriculture attracted 10 times more slugs to beer than to metaldehyde, five times more to unfermented grape juice. Orchid growers have found this is true.

Put a little beer in small saucers placed between the pots or on the greenhouse floor in the evening. Set containers at five-foot intervals. The slugs will come from all directions and drink the beer and drown in it.

If you use poison bait, put it under boards or pots so children, pets and birds (if outdoors) do not get it. Don't put it on the surface of the potting medium unless you put it in a small container like a bottle cap.

Keep your plant area clean of debris, empty pots and other hiding places. If you grow plants beneath your benches or with your orchids in your house, put bait or beer around them.

SUGAR ANTS may be seen on flower buds and stems seeking the nectar that forms with the buds. They may injure the flower tissues in collecting or eating the honey.

Larger ants, if seen on flowers or plants, may be herding mealybugs, aphids or soft scales.

Control of ants: Do not get insecticides recommended for ant control on the flowers. Some ant controls are too strong to apply to foliage or roots. Use ant baits in small containers near the infested plants. Spray or dust the trails, benches, ground beneath benches and greenhouse walls.

CATERPILLARS in variety may infest phalaenopsis, but are not universal or serious on these orchids. Some worms that are pests of other ornamentals and vegetables might appear on orchids.

Caterpillars are the immature stages of butterflies and moths that hatch from eggs laid by the flying mothers on the host plants. Caterpillars may be smooth-skinned or fuzzy. In the Philippines and elsewhere that the hair-streak butterfly is indigenous, its larva is partial to phalaenopsis. This is a pinkish-green caterpillar about ½ inch long at maturity that looks like a slug but may not be a beer drinker.

Control of caterpillars: Hand pick or apply contact insecticide at once.

GRASSHOPPERS, BEETLES, KATYDIDS AND CRICKETS may chew flowers. Hand pick.

ROACHES, large and small of many nationalities, chew jagged hunks out of open blooms at night. Keep poison bait around flowering plants. Place them directly on benches or on bottle caps on the potting medium.

RODENTS: Rats and mice may feast on flowers or pollen. Use standard poisons if you suspect rodents. Do not put directly on the plants.

BEES AND WASPS may be attracted to the flowers and may disturb the pollen, causing blooms to fold up.

THE DISEASES

Two FUNGUS DISEASES may infect phalaenopsis flowers.
European anthracnose (Gloeosporium affine), described under foliage

problems, may occasionally cause spotting of the flowers in infected plants. If blooms are old or of poor quality the tiny brown spots may run together into larger spots and cover the whole flower.

Petal blight (Botrytis cinerea) is a stage of a weak fungus named Sclerotinia fuckeliana. The symptoms are tiny pinprick size brown spots on the blooms, which quickly grow larger and more numerous.

Control of fungus diseases: The first step is to pick and destroy all infected blooms at once to reduce chances of spreading the disease. Apply preventive spray of fungicide specifically recommended for control of botrytis to open blooms at stated intervals. Do not mix it stronger than recommended for flower contact or the flowers may be damaged.

Moving air dries flowers off quickly and helps to prevent the fungus from developing. In an area where air is damp and still and cool the disease is encouraged. If a vent in the top of the greenhouse away from the heater is opened, or some window in a home cracked at a distance from the source of heat, the disease may be lessened. The idea is to pull warm air past the flowers, not to blow a cold draft on them.

This problem is more prevalent when the air is humid and the temperature drops considerably at night. Dry out the air and raise the temperature a little.

MISCELLANEOUS PROBLEMS OF THE FLOWERS

AIR POLLUTION is most likely to affect the buds of phalaenopsis. The most susceptible size seems to depend upon the heredity of the plant. On some phals the little buds less than ¼ inch are the most prone, while on others the buds ⅝ to ¾ inch are likely to be injured at the same time.

Ethylene gas accumulates in the atmosphere during periods of still, cloudy weather, particularly in fall and winter. How much buds are hurt depends on the duration of the exposure and the concentration of the gas. A figure at about 50 parts per billion (ppb) seems to affect the buds, but if it increases to 75 ppb. the recently opened phalaenopsis flowers may fold up one day and become dry soon afterwards.

Buds damaged by ethylene turn yellow within 24-26 hours, stop growing, and several days later they fall off. When they begin to change color and wrinkle you can diagnose the problem but there is little to do about it.

Ethylene gas may accumulate from automobile traffic during periods of smog or fog. It may result from imperfect combustion in a greenhouse or home heater fueled by gas or oil. Unvented heaters are likely to discharge enough ethylene to cause flower damage. A vented heater may not be functioning properly, and a check of the equipment and of the design of the flue may correct the problem. Natural gas is almost free of ethylene.

SEPAL WILT, where dryness first appears on the sepals and heralds wilting may be due to air pollution, ethylene gas, rapid temperature changes, high temperatures and dry air in combination, or poor culture such as too much fertilizer.

FOLDED FLOWERS may be on the way to making seed pods, having been fertilized or disturbed by some insect.

Problems of the Roots

THE PESTS

BUSH SNAILS are tiny flat, round snails about ⅛ inch or less in diameter like a pinhead. They feed on root tips of orchids, and since the green tip is the growing point of the root, its destruction halts growth of root and plant. Then the foliage shrivels or falls off.

Bush snails (Zonitoides arboreus) have become a problem with the widespread use of bark for potting as they thrive in the loose medium and work in the dark moist spaces between the particles. They are brown like the bark and are very difficult to locate down inside the pot and even more difficult to exterminate. They infest all sorts of loose mixes including pumice and gravel.

Their damage mainly eliminates root tips, but sometimes snail damage can be spotted elsewhere on the roots like small brown scars and indentations in the white epidermis. If the snails appear on the surface or chew visible roots, you can identify them quickly. But when they work down in the pot you may not know the infestation is present until the plant is far gone or falls over for lack of anchorage.

Control of bush snails: The incorporation of other materials in the potting mixture, such as fuzzy redwood fiber, makes it more difficult for the bush snails to move through the mixture. Any kind of tight potting material that is suitable for the plants discourages or excludes bush snails.

Snail baits are ineffective with bush snails. Surface sprays eliminate a few at the top but drive others into the depths where you cannot see them.

Repotting to fresh material requires that every bit of old material is cleaned off, the roots dipped in a solution lethal to snails but not to orchids, and the pots sterilized before reuse. Unless you eliminate snails from your entire collection they will be right back.

Present methods favor a drench of 25% diazinon wettable powder (2 tbs. per gallon of water), or an overnight soaking of pots to the rim in a solution of 20% liquid metaldehyde (2 tbs. per gallon of water). Specific recommendations are given because few chemicals control bush snails.

Do not worry about bush snails unless you see them on the surface or when repotting. If a plant is unhappy for no good reason, knock it out of the pot and examine the potting mix and the roots. Keep a close eye on seedlings and community pots.

SLUGS AND SNAILS chew on roots, too. See under Flowers.

ROACHES hide inside pots and chew roots. Use household poison between pots.

ANTS AND TERMITES build nests inside pots, eat roots and cause the medium to break down. If you don't see them but find sawdust, submerge the pot in water to the rim and see what comes scurrying out. Beware of pouring ant poison into the pot unless this is specifically recommended on the brand you buy. Repot, clearing off all old mixture to remove the eggs.

EARTHWORMS hasten the breakdown of the potting mixture which is desirable in garden soil but not in orchid collections. Repot infested plants and relocate the displaced earthworms in the garden.

MILLIPEDES are round worms with many legs and pinkish, brown or grey skin. They infest pots and chew on roots and old potting material. Adults are about an inch long, and when disturbed they coil up like springs. They feed on decaying vegetable matter and manure and are found where plants are rotting but do not cause the rot.

Each female lays 300 eggs in clusters which hatch in three weeks. Young millipedes have only six legs at first and grow slowly so there is usually one generation a year.

Millipedes are unusual in orchids. They are a sign that plants need repotting into fresh material.

SOWBUGS AND PILLBUGS feed on potting mixtures and tender roots. They have oval flat brown bodies with seven pairs of legs. Adults are about ½ inch long. Pillbugs roll up in balls.

These relatives of crayfish breathe through gills. What is more they have pouches like kangaroos in which eggs are laid and where the young live for a while. There is one generation a year. These critters are greenhouse problems in damp places.

Control of sowbugs and pillbugs: You will rarely see them but can recognize them easily. A surface spray or dust of contact insecticide on and around the pots and on the soil beneath greenhouse benches is effective.

SPRINGTAILS are tiny insects like fleas that may appear in large numbers on pot surfaces or around plants. They are grey, milky white or colorful. The common garden springtail is dark purple or black with yellow spots. There are some 2,000 species of springtails in damp places from the Arctic to the Equator. They are all around us but are so tiny we don't notice them. They feed on tender plants and decaying organic matter.

The small insect is about 1/25 inch long with a round body and an oval head. It has no wings and jumps by means of a tail-like appendage.

Control of springtails: Dust or spray with a contact insecticide.

THE DISEASES

A few FUNGUS DISEASES attack roots of phalaenopsis, sometimes spreading to the foliage.

Crown rot or Southern blight (Pellicularia rolfsii), described under foliage problems, shows up as rotting of the roots which may not be noticed except at repotting time. The first symptom may appear when the leaves discolor.

The sclerotia live in potting media for an unlimited length of time, so if you do not wish to destroy the plant, destroy the medium, dip the plant in fungicide, and repot.

Root rot (Pellicularia filamentosa, synonym Rhizoctonia aolani) may be fatal to seedlings. Mature plants may be set back by an infection. Poor drainage of the potting medium is the major cause. Plants that need repotting because the mixture drains slowly and air does not reach the roots should have prompt attention.

A brown mycelium is the most destructive aspect of this fungus. Mycelium is a mass of tangled and interwoven threads that run through the pot.

Because of non-functioning roots, the foliage gradually declines, becoming yellowish, shriveled, and thin. New leaves are progressively smaller instead of larger.

Fusarium wilt (Fusarium oxysporum) is a disease that rots the roots and causes foliage to react the same way it does with root rot. The plant goes into a decline. It may die within a few weeks or struggle along for nearly a year.

Control of fungus root diseases: Remove all medium and remove by hand any signs of mycelium clinging to roots. Cut off dead roots. Dip remaining roots or the whole plant in a fungicide at the specified dilution and duration. Be sure the label recommends that particular product for use on live plants.

Snow mold (Ptychogaster species) is a saprophytic fungus that does not invade the plant but spreads through the potting mixture. It may cover the roots and the base of the plant, but mostly it grows on the bark, tree fern or other medium in the pot. It is resistant to water and so the roots and potting mix get no moisture. Water runs off. Plants decline for lack of water and because roots are smothered.

Control of snow mold: You can see snow mold when you repot or when it emerges from the surface or cracks of a pot. Repot at once, removing all old medium from the roots. Dip roots in fungicide specified for snow mold control.

Friends

Not all bugs are bad. There are estimated to be 700,000 species of insects in the world, but only 1/10 of them are enemies of man. The rest are our friends or they mind their own business.

There are a number of beneficial critters that help to control the pest population where orchids are grown outdoors or in unscreened greenhouses. Try to recognize your friends and avoid harming them when using poison sprays. Systemics applied as drenches do not injure the friends, but insecticides applied as sprays or dusts do.

LADY BEETLES or lady bugs are familiar with their red oval bodies with or without black spots. The larva stage is less well known. It has a jointed body about 1/5 inch long that is tapered at the end.

One lady beetle can eat 50 aphids a day or an equal quantity of spider mites, scales or mealy bugs. She may lay 1,500 eggs a month.

ASSASSIN BUGS are clumsy creatures with hairy legs and over-lapping wings that walk around eating many pests, particularly in immature stages. This helper has adhesive pads on his legs to hold his victim, venom in his head to paralyze it, and suction mouthparts to draw out its tissues. There are about 2,500 species of these little-known bugs and we should know them better.

LACEWINGS are pale green 3/4 inch flies with gossamer oval wings and long antennae and are mothers of aphid-lions. An aphid-lion is an ugly wingless 1/3 inch creature with jaws like a sickle. It eats aphids at the rate of one a minute every day for the two weeks of this stage. Then it rolls up in a cocoon the size of a pea and emerges as an adult that does not eat but lays up to 40 eggs a night. You can recognize the eggs because they stand up on stalks attached to foliage, a device to keep the hatching larvae from eating their siblings.

PRAYING MANTIS, which everybody recognizes with its upright walking-stick body, with the forelegs in a prayerful position, grows two to five inches long. It feeds on many insects including its mate and relatives. It is possible to buy mantis eggs to start a colony.

WASPS may be beneficial. Some catch insects to feed their young. One species of parasitic wasp lays eggs in the bodies of aphids, and when a young wasp is ready to hatch it eats a hole in the host's back.

If you find a dead aphid and look under a hand magnifying glass to see a round hole in its back, you know the friendly wasp is at work.

FROGS, TOADS AND TREE FROGS are busy exterminators who eat their weight in insects. Some of them sit as fat and immobile as Nero Wolfe but they have long sticky tongues that capture anything edible that comes within range.

A tiny green or brown tree frog sings while he patrols a humid growing area.

CHAMELEONS and other lizards are busy all day chasing insects around the greenhouse. A chameleon has two visible eyes and another eye in the back of its head that you cannot see but enabling him to catch up with almost anything that moves. Lucky is the greenhouse owner who has a population of lizards.

OTHER FRIENDS in the outdoors are dragonflies, damsel bugs, spiders, snakes, turtles, beetles and birds.

CHAPTER XIV

DECORATIVE USE
OF ORCHIDS

Phalaenopsis are extremely decorative either as individual blooms or as entire sprays. The stems are graceful and the blooms last for weeks if protected from dry air, cold drafts and strong wind.

Still on the plant you only have to set a pot of phalaenopsis inside a decorative container to have a living flower arrangement in your home. Use a plant with a pendant spray inside a hanging container.

Plant a big strawberry jar with several large white or large pink phalaenopsis and it is gorgeous in bloom. Move it to a position in your home for a magnificent display. Use pots of ferns around the base.

When you bring plants from the greenhouse indoors, take them daily to the kitchen sink for thorough watering and draining.

Cut phalaenopsis spikes are excellent gifts. Buy inexpensive but heavy dime store bud vases, put a single spike in one, alone or with a frond of fern, and you have a perfect token for a hospital, an office, or a hostess.

Phalaenopsis spikes work beautifully into flower arrangements of any style from Oriental and Victorian to contemporary. The spikes have a naturally artistic line which determines the overall design.

In the designs pictured here that were made by Ruby Mack, most of the containers did not hold water. She put the ends of the spikes into tubes of water, and then hid the tubes in the designs.

When you refill a tube, which you must do often, slice a fraction from the end of the stem to open up the passages.

There are hundreds of flower arrangement books and you will find many designs that you can copy using phalaenopsis instead of more common flowers.

Corsages

Phalaenopsis make up into beautiful corsages and bouquets. You can use as many or as few as you wish, depending on the occasion. One flower, with the stem wired and taped for security, accents a dress or a hairstyle. Two or three large flowers make the usual corsage, if small phals are used, five or seven is better.

First be sure the flowers are ripe, which means fully open and mature. If they look floppy on the plant they will look limp when cut. Usually three or four days after opening is suitable for cutting, but of course flowers can be three or four weeks old if they are still fresh.

Pick each flower where the pedicel joins the main stem. Put the stem end in water for a few hours or overnight if possible. You can float it in shallow water and dry it on paper towelling, or you can use a small saucer or ashtray to prop the bloom against the rim with the end of the stem in the water.

Then take a fine corsage wire and shape it into a hairpin. Wrap this wire with tape to match the color of the flower's column. Slightly bend the curve of the hairpin to fit the contour. Put this wire over the column with the ends to the back of the flower between the top sepal and the petals. Hold one side of the wire next to the stem, wrap the other around the stem and the parallel wire. (Sketches A-B-C)

Another method, useful if the petals and sepals overlap so there are no openings for the wires between them, is to insert a short length of corsage wire into the column from the back of the flower. Then bend the wire to the shape of the pedicel. Make a hairpin wire and place it parallel to the stem with the curve against the back of the flower. Keep one side straight and wrap the other around both wires and the flower stem. (Sketches D-E)

Still another way is to make the hairpin, place it in the above position, and wrap one end around the other. (Sketches F-G).

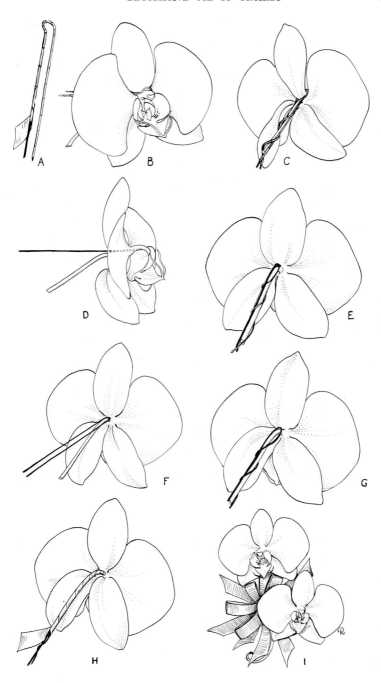

After any wiring procedure cover the stem of each flower with a piece of floral tape. Begin at the top, stretch it as you wrap around and around down the stem. It will stick to itself. I like to wrap the bare stem before wiring, too, but this is optional.

Arrange the flowers in a design and secure each one's stem to the next one with a short piece of flexible corsage wire wrapped around one spot. Cover the wires with tape.

Add ribbon bows, leaves, net or other corsage accessories. Just don't overpower your flowers with trimmings.

Several phalaenopsis corsages are pictured in YOU CAN GROW ORCHIDS.

Boutonnieres

The men who grow orchids ought to wear the small phalaenopsis for boutonnieres. A fresh flower is always a conversation piece, especially when it is an orchid. A man who always wears a boutonniere says it draws comments and questions in the elevator, on the street, and in groups. If he doesn't wear a flower to the office, everybody wants to know why. But when somebody says, "Is that a real orchid?" it opens the way to suggest that person grow orchids, too.

Since most men's coats are made without lapel button holes now, the flower must be pinned on, and so you may find it holds up better if the stem is wrapped with tape, or even if a short piece of hairpin wire is used in the corsage technique. It keeps the pin from breaking the stem.

Floating a flower in water prior to wearing it helps keep it fresh throughout the day, but if you make a quick dash to the greenhouse in the morning, take along a tube of water and put the flower in it while you shave or eat breakfast.

There are any number of nickel and quarter-sized phalaenopsis blooms that are diminutive boutonnieres. The Phal. fuscata hybrids have strong substance and hold up well. The Doritis pulcherrima primary hybrids are a suitable size. Phal. cornu-cervi lasts all day, and most of the Phal. lueddemanniana complex are excellent for masculine boutonnieres. So are flowers of the Phal. equestris group.

Phalaenopsis sprays fit into basic designs. The one at the top includes fresh variegated pittosporum foliage and sprigs of a vine. The one below on driftwood is accented with dried eleagnus leaves and lion's tail pods. Both arrangements by Ruby Mack.

Luzanne (Mrs. J. H. Veitch x Phal. stuartiana) has a cream flower with a few spots, is the size of a quarter and lasts two days. Claudia Creasy (Luedde-violacea x Cinnamon Stick) is a bronze star of suitable size. Pink Minuet (Pink Satin x Phal. equestris) is nickel size, lasts several days when cut and a long time on the plant. There are many more.

A phalaenopsis corsage needs only a little trimming because the flowers are so beautiful.

CHAPTER XV

CLASSIFICATION AND NOMENCLATURE

Amateur growers need not be overly concerned with tribes, subtribes and subfamilies within the orchid family, Orchidaceae, which is one of more than 300 families of flowering plants in the world.

This book is about the genus Phalaenopsis, which Dodson and Gillespie* class in the subfamily Epidendroideae, which includes most of the epiphytic orchids grown in cultivation. In this subfamily are five tribes, and under Tribe Vandeae are nine subtribes. One of these is Vandinae, which includes the genus Phalaenopsis along with Aerides, Angraecum, Renanthera, Trichoglottis, Vanda and others.

So, Phalaenopsis is a genus, and the genus is the first name of a plant: Phalaenopsis amabilis, Phalaenopsis stuartiana, Doritis pulcherrima.

The genus name can be composed of a combination of genera, two or more, depending on the ancestry of the plant: Phalaenopsis and Doritis result in Doritaenopsis. There are rules for naming new combinations.** See chapter on Multigenerics for more combination names.

On the plant tag the genus name is first and the second name indicates the species or hybrid name. Phalaenopsis amabilis is a species

---

* The Biology of the Orchids, published by Mid-America Orchid Congress, Inc. 1967.
** Handbook on Orchid Nomenclature and Registration, International Orchid Commission. 1969.

found growing in the wild although it has been selfed and reproduced far from its natural home. Phalaenopsis mannii and Phalaenopsis amboinensis are both species but when these two are hybridized the result is a hybrid, Phalaenopsis Mambo.

The genus name is written with a capital letter. It can be abbreviated Phal. with a capital and a period.

The species name begins with a small letter, even when derived from a proper name, as in Phal. amboinensis, referring to the island of Amboina, and Phal. sanderiana, named for Mr. Sander. But the hybrid name begins with a capital, as in Phal. Mambo, Phal. Keith Shaffer, and Phal. Sahara Desert.

In botanical writing the genus name and the species name (but not the hybrid name) are printed in italic type. I have chosen not to do this but to use newspaper style of Roman type throughout the text. This applies to the scientific names of the pests and diseases as well. I have used the name Phalaenopsis or the abbreviation Phal. before species names because they are printed in all small letters, but I have often left off the genus name or abbreviation before the hybrids which stand out because of beginning with capital letters.

When the genus name is used alone (without reference to a certain species or hybrid) it is not capitalized, hence phalaenopsis and doritis appear in all small letters in the text. However, when speaking of the genus as a botanical classification, the name begins with a capital and would be written in italics if we were using them. Don't worry about this point.

Following the genus name and species name may come the abbreviation var. for variety, designating certain variations of the plant or flower. Thus Phalaenopsis lueddemanniana var. ochracea indicates a certain form of Phal. lueddemanniana, in this case characterized by the ochre and cream color.

After the varietal name, or after the hybrid name may come one or two names enclosed in single quotes and beginning with capital letters. This is the cultivar epithet which designates one certain clone or plant from all the others of the same name. Every awarded plant has to have a cultivar epithet, and some other plants are given one if they are very fine and need to be distinguished in a collection. Then the award, if any, follows with the name of the organization giving the award. Thus: Phalaenopsis Ruth Wallbrunn 'Patricia', AM/AOS is a hybrid named

Ruth Wallbrunn, Patricia is the cultivar name of that particular plant, and the initials are an Award of Merit from the American Orchid Society. Any stem propagations, meristem propagations or keikis from this plant carry the cultivar name and the award, but the seedlings of it do not. Other examples: Phalaenopsis Best Girl 'Kensington', HCC/AOS; Doritaenopsis Jerry Vande Weghe 'Gleneyrie', HCC/AOS; Phalaenopsis lueddemanniana var. hieroglyphica 'Angela Marie', AM/AOS, this last a species with a varietal name and a cultivar name.

Other organizations giving awards are designated by their initials: RHS for Royal Horticultural Society, as in Phalaenopsis Henriette Lecoufle 'Boule de Neige', FCC/RHS; AOC for Australian Orchid Council; TOSSEA for The Orchid Society of South East Asia, and so on.

Phalaenopsis are no different from other plants, in that there is frequent controversy over which is the right name for a species. This is a matter for botanists and taxonomists, and we amateurs need not take sides.

In this book I have followed the names listed by Herman Sweet in his Revision of the Genus Phalaenopsis[†] with the exceptions designated by the International Registration Authority in December 1970. I have occasionally indicated synonyms in the text for clarity.

Dr. Sweet divides the genus Phalaenopsis into sections, with closely related species[‡] in each section, as follows, with the I.R.A. synonyms in parentheses.

Section PHALAENOPSIS: amabilis, aphrodite (syn. amabilis), sanderiana, leucorrhoda, intermedia (natural hybrid), veitchiana, schilleriana, stuartiana.

Section PROBOSCIDIOIDES: lowii.

Section APHYLLAE: wilsoni, stobartiana

Section PARISHIANAE: parishii, appendiculata.

Section POLYCHILOS: pantherina, cornu-cervi, valentinii, lamelligera, mannii.

---

† Published in the American Orchid Society Bulletin, Volumes 37-38. 1968-69.

‡ Dr. Sweet capitalizes some of these names, an author's privilege. I have followed the Handbook in listing species with small letters. Also I have inserted in parentheses the names recognized by the IRA.

Section STAUROGLOTTIS: equestris, lindeni.

Section FUSCATAE: viridis, fuscata, kunstleri, cochlearis.

Section AMBOINENSES: amboinensis, javanica, micholitzii, gigantea, robinsonii.

Section ZEBRINAE: speciosa, sumatrana, corningiana, pulchra (lueddemanniana), reichenbachiana (fasciata), fasciata, fimbriata, heiroglyphica (lueddemanniana), lueddemanniana, violacea, pallens (lueddemanniana), mariae, modesta, maculata.

Dr. Sweet recognizes the genus Paraphalaenopsis for the tereteleaved species, so they do not appear in his list. But since the IRA considers them Phalaenopsis, we wrote about Phal. denevei, Phal. laycockii, and Phal. serpentilingua.

There are other systems of classification from earlier botanists. The earliest one divided Phalaenopsis into two groups based on petal width and the presence or absence of appendages at the apex of the lip, and these two divisions are often referred to today. EUPHALAENOPSIS includes the wide petalled species and STAUROGLOTTIS the ones with petals equal to or narrower than the sepals.

In botanical writing the genus name is written: "the Genus Phalaenopsis Blume." Blume refers to the man who named it. Sometimes you see a species written "Phalaenopsis cochlearis Holttum" or "Phalaenopsis gigantea J. J. Smith" which refer to the person who named the original plant. We laymen don't include the personal names.

Renanthopsis Moon Shot (Renanthera Brookie Chandler x Phal. serpentilingua) is bright orange and yellow.

PHOTO CREDITS

Color slides on page 80 by Dr. Henry Wallbrunn.

Photos of all flower arrangements plus pictures on pages 51 and 85 by Louis O. Egner.

Photo page 2 courtesy Vacherot and Lecoufle.

ACKNOWLEDGEMENTS

To Ruby Mack (Mrs. Worden E. Mack) for the flower arrangements pictured.

To G. W. Dekle, Dr. L. C. Kuitert and Harry C. Burnett for assistance with the problem chapter.

To those who loaned slides or fresh blooms as models for the color paintings: Dr. Henry Wallbrunn, Shaffer's Tropical Gardens; Fairchild Tropical Garden; Jones & Scully, Inc.; Arthur Freed Orchids, Inc.; and Fennell's Orchid Jungle.

For information: May and Goodale Moir; Herbert Shipman; John Crookshank; James V. Creasy, Jr.; Dr. Thomas J. Sheehan; Frank McClain; and Robert D. Jones.

RECOMMENDED READING:

ORCHIDS, A Golden Nature Guide, by Shuttleworth, Zim and Dillon. Paperback. 160 pages. All color. $1.25

HOW TO GROW ORCHIDS, A Sunset Book. Paperback. $1.95

HANDBOOK ON ORCHID CULTURE, American Orchid Society. Paperback, 76 pages. 1971 edition. $1.00

YOU CAN GROW ORCHIDS
YOU CAN GROW CATTLEYA ORCHIDS
By Mary Noble. See back cover this book.

For Hybrid lists, Register of awards, and Handbook on Orchid Nomenclature and Registration write to American Orchid Society, Botanical Museum of Harvard University, Cambridge, Mass. 02138 USA; or Royal Horticultural Society, Vincent Square, London S.W. 1, England.

For recommended hardcover books and periodicals see previous books in Noble series.

INDEX

Air quality 28
  pollution 28, 128-129
Altitude 16
Anther 33
Ants 115, 116, 127, 130
Aphids 111-112, 115, 116, 125
Arrangements 8, 40, 45, 46, 135-136, 139
Assassin bugs 133
Awards 32-33, 142-143

Beard, Charles L. 6, 27
Bees 116, 127
Beetles (weevils) 112, 115, 116, 127
Boutonnieres 138
Butterfly 116

Callus 31-33
Caterpillars 115, 116, 119, 127
Centipede 115
Chameleons 136
Classification 141-144
Column 30-33
Containers 94-96, 104
Corsages 136-138, 140
Crickets 127
Culture 9-28

Decorative use 135-140
Diseases
  bacterial 119-120-122
  flower 127-128
  foliage 119-124
  fungus 120-122, 127-128, 131-132
  roots 131-132
  virus 123-124
Division 97-99
duPlooy, J. F. 21

Environment 15-28

Fertilizer 25-28
  "violet water" 39
Flowers 29-34
  diseases 127-128
  miscellaneous problems 128-129
  parts 29-34
  pests 116, 125-127
  qualities 32-33
Foliage 10-12
  diseases 119-124
  miscellaneous problems 124
  pests 109-119
Friends 133-134
Frogs and toads 134

Grasshoppers 115-116, 119, 127
Gray, Malcolm 23
Greenhouses 21, 23, 24, 27
Growth 9-28

Houseplants 20-22
Humidity 24-25

Inflorescence 12-13
Insecticide 106

Jones, Jean Paul 24

Katydids 116, 127

Lacewings 133
Lady beetles 133
Leaf 10-12
  (also see "foliage")
Light 18-20
  artificial 20-22
Lip 30-33
Looper 116

Mealybugs 110-111, 115, 116, 125
Media, potting 93-96
Meristem culture 100
Millipede 115

Mites 113-119
Moir, W. W. G. 26, 28, 91
Multigenerics 89-92

Name 35-36
Nomenclature 35-36, 141-144
Novelties 61-78
Nutrients 25-28, 39

Ovary 31

Pedicel 33
Pest controls 106-108
Pests
    flowers 116, 125-127
    foliage 115, 109-119
    roots 115, 129-131
Petals 30-33
Pink phals 46-53
    hybrids 48-53
    striped 51-53
Plant bugs 113, 115
Plant parts 9-14
Pollen 33
Pollination 101
Potting 93-96
Problems 105-132
    identification 105-106
    prevention 108
Propagation 97-103
Praying mantis 133

Repotting 96

Roaches 115, 116, 127, 130
Rodents 116, 127
Roots 13-14
    diseases 131-132
    pests 129
Rostellum 33

Scale insects 108-110, 115
Seeds 100-103
Sepals 29-33, 129
Shipman, Herbert 39
Slugs and snails 115, 116, 119, 126
    bush snails 129-130
Sowbugs and pillbugs 131
Springtails 131
Stem 12
Stem propagation 99-100

Temperature 16-18
Tendrils 30-31, 33
Tepals 30
Terete phals 79-82
Termites 130
Thrips 112, 115, 116, 125-126

Wasps 116, 127, 134
Water 22-23
White phals 35-45
    hybrids 39-43
    colored lips 42-45

Yellow phals 55-60
    hybrids 58-60

INDEX OF SPECIES AND HYBRIDS

PHALAENOPSIS

amabilis 35-39, 65
Amber Sands 73
amboinensis 69, 74
aphrodite (amabilis) 38
Bridesmaid 76
Carnival 72
cochlearis 58, 69, 73

cochlearis x Golden Sands 73
corningiana 58, 69
cornu-cervi 56, 69
denevei 69, 79
Doris 41-42, pink 48-51
Elisabethae 41
equestris (rosea) 44, 53, 68
fasciata 58, 65
fimbriata 68, 78

formosana (amabilis) 38
Frances Roberts 77
fuscata 57, 69
gigantea 65, 70-74
Golden Chief 59
Golden Louis 59
grandiflora (amabilis) 38
Gretchen 71
Harriettiae 66
Helen Kuhn 57
Henriette Lecoufle 2
Hi Boy 63
Hylo 63
Hymen 58, 63, 68
intermedia 43, 44
Janet Ragan 71
Jimmy Arnold 52
Katherine Siegwart 41
leucorrhoda 52
laycockii 81
lindenii 44, 51-52, 68
Lois Jansen 72
Louis Merkel 76
lueddemanniana 53, 56, 61-64, 65, 94
maculata 69, 78
mannii 55-56, 68
mariae 56, 69
Martha 95
Mary Noble - front cover
micholitzii 58, 65
parishii 68, 75
Partris 75
rimestadiana (amabilis) 38
Ruth Wallbrunn 80
Sally Lowrey 43
Samba 14
sanderiana 47, 65
schilleriana 47, 68
Scotti Maguire 6

septentilingua 69, 79-81
Show Girl 42
Spice Islands 80
stuartiana 37, 39, 68
sumatrana 56, 69
Sunset Glow 63
vietchiana 52
violacea 64-67, 69
Zada 49, 77

RELATED SPECIES, HYBRIDS AND MULTIGENERICS

Asconopsis Irene Dobkin 80
Ascovandoritis Sonnhild Kitts 80
Beardara Charles Beard 73
Doritaenopsis 86-87, 92
   Clarence Schubert 87
   Lizanne Galbreath 80
Doritis 83-87
   pulcherrima 83-84
   pulcherrima var. buyssoniana 84-85
   multigenerics 92
Kingiella 88
   decumbens 88
   philippinensis 88
   taenialis 88
   multigenerics 92
Phalaenopsis multigenerics 89-92
Renanthopsis
   Bronze Delight 90
   Ginger McQuerry 80
   Jan Goo 90
Rhynchonopsis Melody 90
Vandaenopsis
   Mem. Mari de Costa 45, 72
   Septentinda 82